PORTRAIT OF NATURE

ALAN COTTRELL

PORTRAIT

OF

NATURE

The World as Seen by Modern Science

.

CHARLES SCRIBNER'S SONS
New York

Copyright © 1975 Alan Cottrell

Library of Congress Cataloging in Publication Data

Cottrell, Alan Howard.
    Portrait of nature.
    Includes index.
    1. Science.   2.   Nature.   I.   Title.
Q172.C67   500   75-837
ISBN 0-684-14355-0

1 3 5 7 9 11 13 15 17 19 V/C 20 18 16 14 12 10 8 6 4 2

Printed in the United States of America

CONTENTS

CONTENTS

PREFACE

My aim in this book was laid down years ago by William Blake:

> To see a World in a grain of sand,
> And a Heaven in a wild flower,
> Hold Infinity in the palm of your hand,
> And Eternity in an hour.

In these utilitarian days of science we forget that there is another side to it, the visions of a strange and beautiful nature, the rays of light cast on the great dark, the hope of knowing who and where we are. And in these professional days of science we also forget that this should be a picture open to everyone, if it so pleases them. I have thus tried, in this book for the general non-scientific reader, to look through the dense jungle of technical scaffolding at the breathtaking structure that is beginning to take shape behind it, the portrait of nature as seen by science.

It is a pleasure to thank Edward Bevan and Martin Lovett who read some chapters in draft and were most generous and helpful in their comments.

ALAN COTTRELL

PORTRAIT OF NATURE

I

The Great Canvas

Space and Time

Curiosity makes scientists of us all. Some indulge it more deeply than most, but we all start the same. Every child of Adam, still hankering for the Tree of Knowledge, discovers the world all over again, for himself. Groping blindly and instinctively, he touches and learns the feel of things. As the world clears before his eyes he discovers, tremendously, that seeing and touching can go together, which makes things *real*. Then he learns the spacing of things. Reaching for one bright light, he grasps his shining spoon. Reaching for another, he misses the sun.

Gradually it all settles into knowledge. A speck of sand or salt, marvellously small, inspires the idea of a point, something that is there but takes up no space. A hair is just as wonderfully fine, but in one way is quite big. The line stretching out in one direction is different from the point. A sheet of paper seems different again, something big in two directions, a surface. And then there are the real bodies, his toys, the chairs and tables, even himself, big in all directions. They have volume. And there it stops. A row of beads, like points, can be laid out to make a line. Matchsticks can be placed side by side to make a sheet. Sheets of paper can be piled on one another to make a volume. But however much he piles his bricks or other bodies together, he can only make things of bigger volume, not something beyond volume. And so he gradually becomes aware of the 'threeness' of *space*, its three and only three dimensions which on Earth we usually call breadth, depth and height. The series *point, line, surface, volume*, stops at volume where all the available dimensions of space are already brought into play.

But there are other excitements. He will have discovered that things can move about, including himself! Motion brings in the idea of *time*, which is both more simple and more mysterious than space. It is simpler because time has only one dimension. Suppose that we are given a heap of jumbled-up snapshots of a sprint race. By trial and error we find close similarities between certain pictures and eventually succeed in sorting them all out into a single sequence along which the whole course of the race unfolds systematically. Each picture (except the two end ones) then has two and only two neighbours, which show the events immediately before and immediately after itself. This is called a *linear* or *one-dimensional* sequence, since each point of a line has two and only two immediate neighbours, one on each side of it. Time is then the name given to *position* along this sequence of events.

And so we live in a *four-dimensional* 'space-time' world; three of space plus one of time. A *point* in this is no longer an ideally small speck of matter, but one mere *event* in the lifetime of that speck. The speck itself extends all along a line, its *world-line*, which marks its existence in space-time, and its collision is the point where its world-line crosses and touches that of another speck. This four-dimensional picture is forced on us by the continuous existence of bodies. I cannot believe that the table on which I write is swept away, at every instant, and replaced by another one, exactly similar to it. It is surely always the same one! But this means that it extends in time as well as in space. It has endurance, breadth, depth and height. We take these things for granted in ordinary life and often find it convenient to mix up ideas of space and time, as if all four dimensions were the same. We use the words 'long' and 'short' equally to describe both lengths and times. 'How far to the next town?' asks the motorist; 'Only ten minutes', comes the answer; 'Thank goodness, it has been a long day', he replies.

The four-dimensional picture does not come easily, however, because time is so different from space. We can measure the size of a table in space, by sliding a measuring rod over it, but there is no way of sliding a 'duration' up and down the time axis. Each instant of time seems to come to us from the future, is now here fleetingly, and then is gone beyond recall. The only way we can believe that one second of time is as long as another is through the 'principle of lack of sufficient reason', i.e. we can see no reason why a well-made clock should not go through its similar cycles in exactly the same way; and through the consistency with which different well-made clocks of all kinds keep in step with one another.

We do not see the four-dimensional world as a whole, then, but as a series of instantaneous images or 'snapshots', each at an instant of our own time which we call 'now'. This is the familiar way in which we slice through space-time. But there are others. A time-lapse photograph of a busy road at night is a two-dimensional picture of a slice parallel to the time axis, in which the car headlamps are seen as ribbons of light. Duchamps' famous painting 'Nude descending a Staircase' is another example.

Celestial Spheres

To see the world in all its glory, we look up to the sky: The sun and moon, the wandering planets, the great constellations of fixed stars in slow procession across the night sky, the inky depths of space – all these are a source of wonder that has inspired some of man's finest and most imaginative works of poetry and science. The Egyptians and Babylonians, fifty centuries ago, were already skilled astronomers, with good star maps and accurate calendars.

We speak of the 'celestial sphere' and indeed it does appear like an enormous hollow dome, bedecked with golden stars, that is slowly rotating round the earth at its centre. Most of the ancients, believing man to be privileged with a special place at the centre of everything, started from this picture but then could not easily account for the individual and apparently complicated movements of the sun, moon, and planets. Copernicus (1473–1543) swept both the privilege and the complexity away, in one stroke, by showing that the movements we see require only that the earth spins like a top, about its north-south axis, once a day, and that the planets and earth rotate quite simply in (almost) circular paths, each at its own distance and speed, all around the sun. It is almost as if we were looking out at everything from a swivelling chair on a rotating turntable. Copernicus's ideas not only revolutionised astronomy; they also profoundly influenced the general philosophical outlook and scientific view of things, particularly the appeal to the criterion of simplicity, the recognition that the position and motion of one body can be judged only *relatively* to another, and the abandonment of our privileged place in the universe.

Today, we have beautiful photographs to show us that the earth is a ball, floating in space and bathed in sunlight, like the other planets. We can also see its roundness directly, by looking across a calm sea on a clear day to distant ships or shoreline, whose lower parts are hidden 'over the horizon' behind the water's rim. Again, the midday sun lies lower in the southern sky the more northerly we stand, showing that the earth curves away towards the pole. In fact, by measuring the difference in the angle of the midday sun, or the pole star, as seen from two places a known distance apart along a north–south line, we can find how much the earth curves over this distance, and so work out the size of the earth. The ancient Greeks did this. Eratosthenes in about 200 BC noticed that at times when the overhead sun shone to the bottom of a deep well at Aswan, it cast a shadow at Alexandria, 500 miles to the north. From its angle and

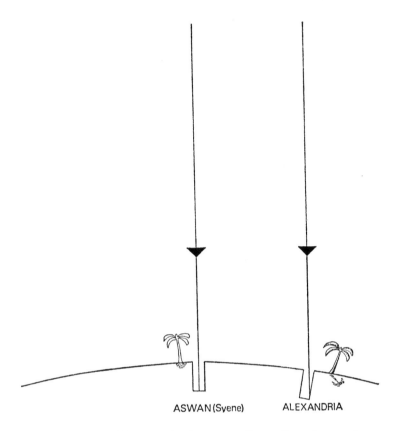

ASWAN (Svene)   ALEXANDRIA

The midday sun shines to the bottom of a well at Aswan but not at Alexandria, 500 miles to the North. From its angle there, and the distance between these two places, the roundness and size of the earth were first determined.

this distance he worked out the size of the earth. We now know that the earth, which is slightly flattened at the poles, has an average radius of about 6400 kilometres (1000 km. = 621 miles).

The earth's axis of spin is not quite at right angles to the plane (called the ecliptic) in which it, along with most of the other planets, sweeps round the sun; it leans $23\frac{1}{2}$ degrees to one side. As a result, the northern hemisphere faces slightly towards the sun during one half of the year – summer time

– and equally away from it during the other half. Without this procession of the seasons, the annual cycle of time would be much less obvious.

The measurement of angles can also tell us how far things are from us, out in space. The method is exactly that also used on earth, by surveyors, and depends on the properties of triangles. First, a straight 'baseline' is measured, by laying out standard rods between two chosen landmarks.

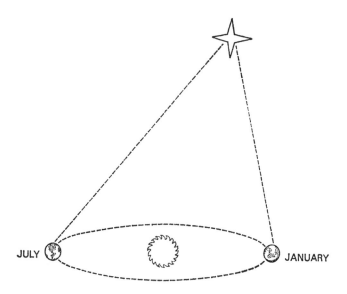

The distance of a nearby star can be found from a knowledge of the diameter of the earth's orbit and a measurement of the star's angles of sighting from the earth at half-yearly intervals. The difference in these angles is greatly exaggerated in the diagram.

Then, from each landmark, the distant object is sighted and the angle its line of sight makes with the baseline is measured. The two points of view give slightly different angles. Since light travels in straight lines, the two lines of sight and the baseline make a triangle whose dimensions can all be worked out from the angles and length of baseline. This is known as the method of *parallax* and it gave the ancients a good idea of the distance of the moon, now known to be just over

380,000 km. The distance of the sun was more difficult because the accurate measurement of a long thin triangle from a short baseline is difficult, but improvements to the method have shown that the sun is about 150 million km. away. Knowing this, it was then easy to find the diameter of the sun (nearly 1,400,000 km.) from the visible size of its disc. A marvellous enlargement of the parallax method also became possible once the distance of the sun was known, because the *earth itself*, at two opposite points in its path round the sun, provided two landmarks having a baseline of 300 million km. The distances of the planets from the sun were then easily found: in millions of km. they are, Mercury (58), Venus (108), Earth (150), Mars (228), Jupiter (778), Saturn (1427), Uranus (2870), Neptune (4497), and Pluto (5950).

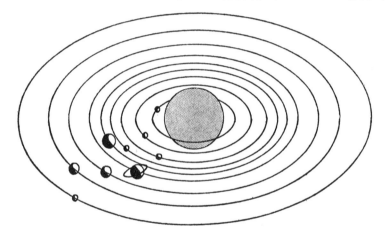

The solar system. From the centre outwards the planets are Mercury, Venus, Earth, Mars, The Asteroid Belt, Jupiter, Saturn, Uranus, Neptune, Pluto.

The 'fixed' stars are much farther away. By eye, we notice no seasonal change in their relative positions. They are mere points of light, even under powerful telescopes, and they twinkle because their beams of light are so fine that they are deflected by minor specks of irregularity in the atmosphere. At its best, parallax can measure out to about 5000 million

million km. which takes in a number of nearby stars, such as the brilliant Sirius (82 million million km.). Most of the bright stars which mark out the great constellations Orion, Andromeda, and the Great Bear or Plough, etc. are 'local' objects. That is why they appear so bright and we notice them. They are our next-door neighbours in space. Farther out, billions of stars exist in the Milky Way, which is our local star 'city' or *galaxy*, and in other great galaxies, far away. Their distances can be found only by less direct methods, such as by comparing brightnesses. Fortunately there are some stars of an easily identifiable type, called Cepheid variables, which all give out the same amount of light. They are like standard light bulbs sprinkled through the universe. We know the distance of the nearest ones by parallax measurements, and can deduce that of the others by their relative brightnesses as they appear to us. Later, we will return to the question of the incredibly vast size of the universe and see that space and time are deeply intertwined; for when we look far out into space we also look far back in time.

Ancient Times

To look back a long way in time, here on earth, the method also is to look back through space, in this case inwards, to the record of the rocks as studied by archaeologists, palaeontologists and geologists. A glance at a cliff or quarry face shows that the rock is stratified in largely horizontal layers like an onion. Near the surface, at archaeologically interesting sites, may be found remains of our own ancestors buried amongst the accumulated debris of the ages, in sand and soil. The underlying rocks themselves fall into three types, igneous, sedimentary and metamorphic. The igneous rocks were formed by solidification from the molten state, as for example when lava is ejected from a volcano, and metamorphic rocks are those originally of any type whose structure has subsequently been changed by heat or pressure. The sedimentary rocks are particularly interesting, having been formed from beds of mineral grains swept together by the weathering actions of wind and water. They were usually deposited in several distinct layers, so that by digging down through them we dig back into the earth's past, and they carry in them the fossilised remains of the ancient fishes, animals and plants that were living at the time they were formed.

What, then, do we know of the age of the earth? Bishop Ussher, in the 17th century, reckoned from the Bible that the Day of Creation was Sunday, 23 October, 4004 B C. If we regard the Bible as history and work backwards, the narrative does in fact run out at roughly about 4000 B C. But some biblical cities such as Ur and Jericho are now known to be many centuries older than this.

Classical geology divided the history of the earth into four main ages. Working backwards from today these are first the Quaternary era, which takes in the age of man and the great glacial periods, then the Tertiary during which the land was largely covered with trees and many of the mountain masses familiar today were formed. Before this was the Mesozoic era dominated by the great prehistoric reptiles, and preceded in turn by the Paleozoic era which goes backwards from the time of the early sea creatures to the pre-Cambrian times of the first lands and seas. The order of these eras and the various phases of their evolution were worked out in great detail, but the fixing of their precise dates proved more difficult. The saltiness of the oceans, due to the slow wash of soluble substances into them from the rocks, by the rivers, showed by calculation that the earth was at least 90 million years old, and estimates of the earth's cooling from the measured loss of heat from the hot core showed that at least 20 million years had elapsed since a solid crust was formed. But the real evidence came from radioactivity, the process by which chemical elements become fundamentally transformed, the nature of which we shall consider later. The naturally radioactive processes that take place in the earth give off heat and, when the amount of this heating was realised, it became plain that the previous figures for the time of the earth's cooling were hopeless underestimates. It also became clear that the sun maintains its heat, and has done so for thousands of millions of years, by the thermonuclear type of radioactive processes. Analysis of rocks, on earth, on meteorites and on the moon, for their composition of radioactive substances has given more precise information and it is now quite certain that the earth and the solar system are about 4600 million years old. This seems to be about one-third of the way back, in the age of the universe as a whole, so that we belong to a fairly young star. In place of Bishop Ussher's estimate we now have, on the basis of cosmological considerations (Chapter 3) and also from analysis of the development of old stars in certain globular clusters, a date for the birth of the universe as somewhere between ten and twenty thousand million years ago. The day and month are no longer certain.

Something very important for us is the *stability* of our corner of the universe, for steady conditions over many hundreds of millions of years must have been needed for life to evolve. The study of daily and yearly growth rings on fossil corals, going back about 600 million years, has shown that the year then was not much different from that now, consisting of about 425 days whose length was nearly 21 of today's hours. The earth's motion has undergone only slight changes over all that time, the most noticeable of which is a slow change in the direction of its spin axis, taking about 26,000 years to go round a circular path which takes in the direction of the pole star to which it happens to point at present ('precession of the equinoxes'). Other than this, the motion hardly changes from year to year. We are fortunate in living in a quiet part of the universe, on a satellite of a star which, although of a common and undramatic type, by astronomical standards, nevertheless belongs to a family noted for its steadiness and longevity.

2

Travels in Space-Time

Light and Colour

The long struggle to find how far it is to the stars – only rewarded when Bessel detected stellar parallax in 1838 – led astronomers in the 17th century to a quite different discovery, a small yearly cycle in the apparent positions of the stars. Bradley (1729) explained this motion, now called *aberration*, by supposing that light does not travel instantaneously. The speed of the astronomer, riding on earth round the sun at 30 km. per sec., across the paths of this starlight, could then alter the angle at which the rays seem to come in, just as vertical rain seems angled towards one's face when driving through it.

Even before this, Roemer (1675) deduced the speed of light from an apparently odd behaviour of a moon of Jupiter's. This moon seemed to get later in its orbit at those times when the earth, moving round the sun, swung away from Jupiter; and to get earlier as the earth swung back again. Roemer realised that this was simply due to the fact that the news of that moon's position took longer to reach us when its light had to cross the extra distance of the earth's orbit round the sun. The modern value of the speed of light, from measurements here on earth, is almost exactly 300,000 km. per sec.

This is enormous, by everyday standards. We know of no faster messenger than light. No wonder that it seems to go instantaneously. It takes only $1\frac{1}{4}$ seconds to get here from

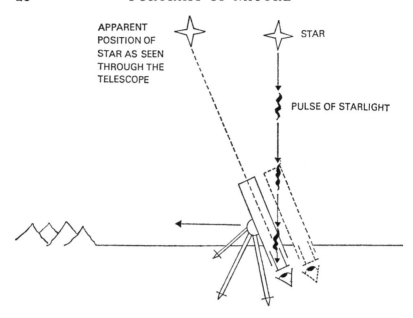

A star is viewed by a telescope which is moved across the line of sight by the earth's motion. While a pulse of starlight is travelling down the telescope tube, the telescope moves sideways, as shown (exaggerated!). In order that the pulse shall reach the eyepiece, the telescope has to be inclined slightly in the direction of the earth's motion. Because of this inclination, the star appears to be shifted, in this same direction. This is *Aberration.*

our moon, and 8 minutes from the sun. Even so, the fact that it is not infinitely fast means that we are always looking at the past. We never see the present.

And for the stars, this past goes back years. In fact the *light-year*, the nearly 10 million million kilometres travelled through space by light in one year, is a popular measure of astronomical distance. Even the nearest star is about $4\frac{1}{2}$ light-years away; and the most remote objects are seen only as they were some thousands of million years ago. When we look out at the night sky we are thus looking at a space-time slice through the universe, outwards in space towards the limits of the universe and backwards in time towards its beginning.

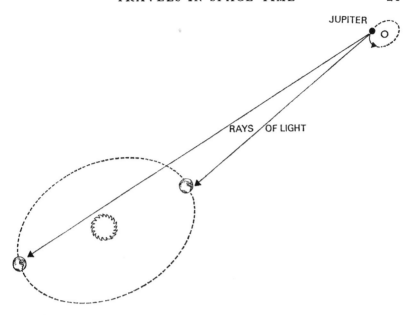

The news of the position of Jupiter's moons reaches us later, when the earth and Jupiter are on opposite sides of the sun, than when they are on the same side. From this fact, Roemer deduced the speed of light.

But what is light, anyway? This is one of the oldest questions in science and still has mysteries for us today. Newton's starting point was the beautiful *spectrum* of colours produced when light is deflected through glass prisms as in chandeliers, or in the iridescence of soap films or flash of diamonds, or in a rainbow. He showed that a beam of 'white' light is a bundle of rays of the various spectral colours and that it is split up and opened out into a fan of separate coloured rays by passing through a prism, which bends rays of different colours through different angles. He showed also that the colours of paints and flowers are mixtures of pure spectral colours. A bright red flower, for example, looks red in white light because it absorbs more light at the blue end of the spectrum and reflects more at the red end; and it looks black in spectral blue light.

Newton thought from these effects that light might be a kind of *wave* motion but nevertheless felt doubtful because it travels in straight lines, like fast bullets, whereas waves tend to spread out in all directions. The decisive evidence came from Young (1801) who, ironically, worked from an effect that Newton had already seen in water waves. If you throw two stones simultaneously, a few feet apart, into a still pond the circular ripples from each spread out and cross through those from the other. At each point on the surface where ripples overlap, each adds itself wholly to the other (called *linear superposition*) so that two equal crests make a hump of double height where they cross; two troughs make a hollow of double depth; and a crest and trough cancel each other out so that the water stays level there. The layout of enhanced and cancelled regions produced by this interference of overlapping waves is called a *diffraction pattern*.

Light shows this. If you look at a distant point of light through an umbrella or a silk screen – the mesh must be fine because light waves are closely spaced, i.e. they have short *wavelengths* – you will see the central spot of light surrounded by a symmetrical pattern of fainter spots. This is the diffraction pattern. As the rays go through the holes of the mesh they are scattered in all directions. Mostly, the crests and troughs cancel, in this jumble of criss-crossing rays, i.e. we have light adding to light to give darkness! But in a few special directions the distances from the holes all differ exactly by zero, one, two, or more exact wavelengths, and along these directions the rays neatly fit together, crest to crest and trough to trough, giving sharp bright beams of light.

Knowing the angles of these diffracted rays and the spacing of the mesh (or *diffraction grating*) the wavelength of the light can easily be found. The range is from about 13,000 waves per centimetre for red light to about 30,000 for violet. The *frequencies* of these waves are very high, by comparison with those, say, of audible sound waves (e.g. middle C is

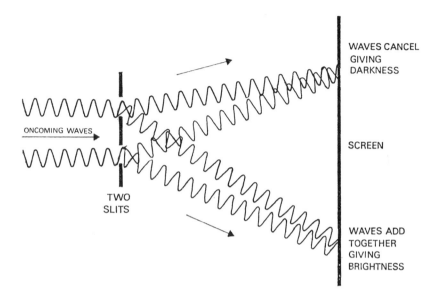

ONCOMING WAVES

TWO
SLITS

WAVES CANCEL
GIVING
DARKNESS

SCREEN

WAVES ADD
TOGETHER
GIVING
BRIGHTNESS

Waves pass through two slits and go on in various directions towards a screen. Their behaviour along two such directions is shown. In one direction the angle is such that the waves from each slit fit together, crest to crest, where they overlap and in this case they reinforce each other to give a bright place on the screen. In the other direction they cancel each other out, crest against trough, where they overlap and the screen there is dark. Similar *constructive* or *destructive interference* of the waves occurs in other directions, so that a *diffraction pattern* of alternate bright and dark places is formed on the screen.

261 cycles of vibration a second). For instance, green light contains about 20,000 waves per cm.; moving at 300,000 km. per sec. it thus makes 600 million million oscillations a second. Shorter waves have even higher frequencies.

We now know that the visible spectrum is only a section of a vast range of radiations which differ only in their wavelengths or frequencies. Going away from the visible spectrum, at the long wave end, there are first the *infra-red* rays, then the *micro-waves* of radar, and finally the long *radio* waves, with wavelengths going up to thousands of metres. The short-wave end starts with the ultra-violet, goes on to *X-rays* – about 100 million waves to a centimetre – and thence to the even shorter *gamma rays*. But all of these radiations are of the same basic type. They all spread outwards as a series of oscillations from a source, at the same universal speed of 300,000 km. per sec. in empty space. They can all be channelled along a narrow beam, provided that the width of the beam is large compared with the wavelength so that rays deviating appreciably from the general direction of the beam cancel out through the criss-crossing of various crests and troughs. We also know now that they are all *transverse* vibrations; that is, their oscillations take place in directions at right angles to the beam, rather like the waves passed along a suspended rope by waving one end sideways.

Window on the World

Light enriches our world with colour. We enjoy a fine blue daytime sky and admire magnificent red sunsets. The move-ments of the air, on a minute scale, produce small fluctua-tions of density which cause some sunlight to be scattered as it passes through. The red and yellow rays, having longer wavelengths, are able – like a large boat on the sea – to ride through these irregularities without much disturbance, as we also know from the effectiveness of fog lamps. But the short-wave blue rays are more sensitive and get thrown in every direction all over the daytime sky. In the evening we see the reddened sun at the end of a long line of sight through the atmosphere, from which blue rays have been filtered out, by scattering, to make someone else's daytime sky. These are of course all earthly pleasures; a few dozen kilometres above us, in the void beyond our atmosphere, the spaceman sees the sun in a black sky.

Light and its companion radiations also bring us rich information about the universe; about the stars, their temperatures, sizes, and compositions; about the regions between the stars; and the sizes and shapes of the galaxies and how they are spread through space. A very familiar effect gives the temperature. When a piece of coal – or iron, stone, or other material – is heated to incandescence, the light it gives out not only brightens strongly as the temperature goes up; it also changes colour, from dull red at first, to bright red, orange, yellow, white and eventually 'electric' blue-white. All hot opaque bodies more or less show the same colours at the same temperatures, which is why, for example, a red-hot poker, embedded in red-hot coals, seems to merge into its background. This colour change can be studied systematically in *spectroscopes*, which spread the light out into its spectrum and enable the temperatures of the surfaces of stars to be found. The sun, at about 6000° Centigrade, is fairly average; others range from 3000° c to 30,000° c. These are not exceptionally high by our standards, e.g. compared with a welding torch; but deep inside the stars it is another matter, for the amounts of light that pour out imply temperatures well above 10 million° c there.

The stars vary enormously in visibility. Mostly, this is simply because some are much farther away than others, but even when this is allowed for, there remain great differences. Some stars are hotter than others of course, but even those of the same colour often show great differences in brightness. The remaining factor is *size*, which can be deduced from the brightness, after correcting for the other effects. Stars vary greatly in both size and intrinsic brightness; most fall in a 'main sequence' running from cool, big, *red giants* to small, hot, *white dwarfs*. The sun, a yellow star with a radius of about 700,000 km., is a middling star in this sequence.

The clues to the chemistry of the universe come from another feature of starlight. Early in the 19th century it was noticed that the spectra of the sun and stars are crossed at certain wavelengths with fine lines, which could be reproduced in the laboratory by adding chemicals, such as salt, to flames under spectroscopic examination. Each chemical element such as hydrogen, oxygen, sodium, etc. in fact produces a unique set of spectral lines, a marvellous 'fingerprint' for detecting it throughout the universe; and the intensities of the lines can tell us how much of it there is.

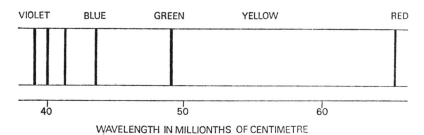

Lines produced by hydrogen at certain wavelengths in the optical spectrum.

The sun and stars have similar compositions, being almost all hydrogen, having about one atom in ten of helium, and a trace of everything else, in great contrast to the earth and inner planets. It is good to know that most of the sun's fuel – hydrogen – is still unused and will see us through aeons of time. We have learned a lot about the distribution of hydrogen in the universe from the fact that it produces a very clear signal in the radio range of the spectrum, which has given radio-telescopes an extra window on the world. Spectroscopy has also shown that space itself, between the stars, is not completely empty. There is extremely rarefied gas, roughly as if a cube of our ground-level atmosphere were stretched out a few million times along each side. Most of this interstellar gas is hydrogen and helium, but with traces of other substances including some fascinating organic molecules discovered recently by radio-astronomers, as well as occasional grains of dust.

When astronomers turned their spectroscopes on the more distant galaxies, about 50 years ago, they found the familiar

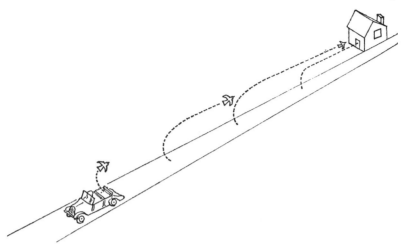

A man drives away from home at a steady speed. At the end of each hour he releases a pigeon which flies home at this same speed. Each arrives home two hours after the one before it. The frequency of their arrival home, i.e. one every two hours, is thus *lower* than the frequency of their release, i.e. one every hour. This is an example of the *Doppler effect*. If the car had beamed back light waves instead of pigeons, the frequency of these waves would have been similarly (but slightly) lowered towards the red end of the spectrum, so giving a *red shift*.

spectral lines, but shifted extraordinarily towards the red end of the spectrum. We now know that this *cosmological red shift* is basically the same effect as when a train whistle drops in pitch through rushing past us; each successive wave comes to us from a point farther away than the one before it, and so the distance between waves is stretched in proportion to the speed of the source away from us, thus increasing the wavelength and lowering the frequency (*Doppler effect*). The speeds of these galaxies, away from us, are enormous. For example, a cluster of galaxies in the constellation Hydra, estimated from their brightness to be almost 2200 million light-years away, are retreating at over 60,000 km. a second. Radio-astronomy has taken us still farther, revealing galaxies strongly emitting radio-waves (*radio-galaxies*) at distances of 5000 million light-years moving away at half the speed of light, and other small-diameter but extremely powerful radio emitters (*quasars*) with red shifts equivalent to more than 90 per cent of the speed of light and distances which may exceed 9000 million light-years.

We see very much the same, whichever direction we look out into space beyond the Milky Way; and the speeds at which the galaxies are retreating (apart from small local variations) increase regularly with distance in such a way that, if we divide the distance by the speed, we get the same answer, a time of about 18,000 million years, for every galaxy. A figure of roughly this value turns up in various ways as the characteristic time or 'age' of the universe.

We might be tempted by all this to think that we are back in a privileged place again, at the centre of things, with everything else moving away from us symmetrically in all directions. But not so. Sprinkle dots of paint on a sheet of rubber and then stretch this rubber equally in all directions, as for example when we blow up a balloon. Anyone sitting on any dot will see all the others moving symmetrically away from him; and exactly the same thing is seen from every other dot.

This is the famous discovery of the *expanding universe*. Given remarkable foresight it might have been anticipated centuries ago from the simplest of all astronomical observations: that the night sky is black. Olbers (1826) was the first to realise that this contained a great clue to the universe. He asked, why should it be black, if the universe and stars go on for ever, in all directions: for in that case, *every* line of sight out into the sky should end up on a star, sooner or later, so that the whole sky should be as bright as the sun at all times. But a finite age of a few thousand million years, or equivalently an overwhelming red shift and weakening of the light coming to us from a few thousand million light-years away, is well able to give us a dark sky.

It seems likely that there are over 1 million million galaxies in the universe, often grouped in small clusters which themselves seem to be spread fairly evenly in all directions and at all distances. Our galaxy, the Milky Way, is an example of the common type of *spiral galaxy*. Its 10,000 million stars are arranged partly in a central cluster, about 2000 light-years in diameter, and partly in spiral arms which wind out from it so that it looks rather like a Catherine-wheel about 100,000 light-years in diameter. The sun is in one of the spiral arms, about 35,000 light-years from the centre.

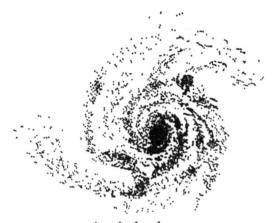

A spiral galaxy.

The whole galaxy is rotating, relative to the universe of galaxies, the centre faster than the outside, and the sun and its local companions take about 250 million years to go round once. So much for the 'fixed' stars! We are moving at about 250 km. a second relative to the universe, due to this rotation.

Coasting through Space

We find a universe full of movement. Stars streaming round their galaxies; galaxies rushing apart at speeds almost up to that of light itself; all as seen from the light they send us. And yet we have been supposing that whenever we measure the speed of light, we always get the same answer, 300,000 km. a second (in space); and 'always' means that it doesn't matter whether the source is moving or we are moving, or both. How can this be? There is in fact something very odd about the motion of light and to understand this we must look first at motion generally.

In these days of space travel, 'weightlessness' is a familiar fact even though few have experienced it. When its rockets are switched off, above the atmosphere, a space ship coasts along effortlessly. Everything inside it, including the spacemen, coasts along with it, feeling not the slightest push or pull in any direction. Even though near the earth or moon, and not far from the sun, there is no sense of gravity, although the ship is guided by their gravitational influence and moves in a curved orbit, round the earth or looping out to the moon. If the ship were to go off into outer space, away from the planets, sun and other stars, these 'local' gravitational influences would gradually weaken and it would eventually find itself moving at uniform speed in a straight line (e.g. as indicated by a fixed aberration of the stars). This is freely coasting motion at *constant velocity*.

Motion is thus basically an effortless activity – things tend to go on as they are, moving steadily without need for rocket firings or anything else – and the effortless motion of bodies free from external influences takes place at constant velocity. We owe this *law of inertia*, one of the most profound discoveries about our world, to the genius of the early physicists, culminating in Galileo and Newton, who extricated its basic simplicity from the maze of complex effects and false clues belonging to motions here on earth, where there is strong local gravity, air resistance which slows everything down, and other influences from the earth's rotation. But we get some experience of it when we drink tea in a train. This is an orderly activity, not significantly different from that at home, when the train is running smoothly at constant speed along a straight track. The laws of mechanics, which govern the pouring and drinking of tea, are clearly not affected by the constant velocity. Any such velocity can simply be added to all the motions of a mechanical system without producing any changes in the internal behaviour of the system. In this sense, velocities are purely *relative*.

But, does this relativity mean that we can use different values for the velocity of light, simply by adding on whatever velocity we think that we, or its source, or both, may have? No, we cannot. For example, the speed of light, coming to us from pairs of stars rotating round each other, shows no change as one star swings towards or away from us in circling its companion. And accurate local measurements on earth of the speed of light along and across the earth's path round the sun, show no influence of the earth's own movements. The value is always the same.

There thus seems to be a great contradiction between two aspects of the world: the relativity of velocities in general, and the absoluteness of the velocity of light in particular. Einstein's great contribution in his *Special Theory of Relativity* was to force through with iron logic the shattering change in our ideas of space and time needed to reconcile these two seemingly incompatible facts.

The Speed Limit

To see this, imagine someone in an airliner, eating a meal as it flies over us. He stabs a sausage and raises it to his mouth. These two events are, for him, a mere 20 centimetres and 1 second apart; but for us, on the ground watching the plane fly past, the sausage travelled about 200 metres while on its last journey. Now enliven this little story with some science fiction. What if sausages always travelled at the same speed, 20 cm. per sec., as seen by *everyone*? We would then have to say that the man in the plane took 1000 seconds, by our reckoning, to raise his sausage; and since he would be equally sure that it took only one of his seconds, we would have to say that his clock was going only one-thousandth as fast as ours.

Absurd, of course. But just this happens when pulses of light are used, in place of sausages. Of course, light goes

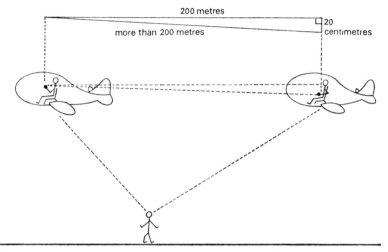

The man in the plane raises a sausage 20 centimetres but to the man on the ground it flies more than 200 metres. If it were a pulse of light, which goes always at the same speed for everyone, the time of its journey would appear much longer to the man on the ground, who would conclude that time was going slowly in the plane.

immensely faster, so that the plane would hardly have moved while the light was travelling its 20 cm. across it. The difference in time rates would then be almost imperceptible. But it would still be there. Moreover, it is quite feasible scientifically (although technically beyond our means) to have a super-plane going so fast above the atmosphere that it moves 200 metres during the light's journey. In this case we really would have to conclude that, by our time-keeping, things in that plane were happening very slowly. But the man in the plane would notice nothing strange about his circumstances, because everything inside the plane would be happening *consistently*. All its clocks would be keeping time together, his pulse would be pacing them normally, people would be moving about, talking and eating sausages as usual, and light would flash around the cabin at its standard speed. We would have to say then, that not any particular process, but all of them, that is *time itself*, was going slowly inside that plane, by our reckoning. This is Einstein's famous *time dilatation*, which Shakespeare anticipated 300 years earlier as 'time travels in divers paces with divers persons'.

No material body can go as fast as light. At first, this seems obviously wrong. Surely the light went only 20 cm. while the super-fast plane went 200 metres? No; such a statement mixes up two quite different sets of observations. The man who sees the light move only 20 cm. is the man in the plane, and relative to him the plane is at rest! We on the ground see the plane move 200 metres, but we also see the light move that same 200 metres and, at the same time, also move 20 cm. across the flight path. In fact the light goes along the *hypotenuse* of a right-angled triangle, the other two sides being in this case 200 metres and 20 cm. long, and we know from Pythagoras that the hypotenuse squared is equal to the *sum* of the squares of the other two sides. Whether the plane goes slowly, fast or super-fast, the light always goes a bit farther, in the eyes of any given observer. And since the speed of light is always the same, the plane – or any other material body – can never go quite as fast as this. It is nature's speed limit.

How real is all this? Notice first that the effects are symmetrical. The man in the plane, seeing our scene rushing past him below, would be struck by how slowly we were going about our affairs. Is it then all merely an appearance, as when two men each see the other apparently getting smaller as they walk apart? No; it can produce real and permanent effects. There is for example a certain type of small particles (now called muons) which are produced out of collisions between other particles and which then 'live' for only a short while before they break up into something else. At rest in the laboratory they live for about two millionths of a second (two microseconds). If there were no time dilatation the farthest they could travel, even at the speed of light, would be only about 0.6 km. However, these same particles are also produced at the top of our atmosphere,

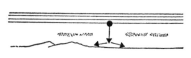

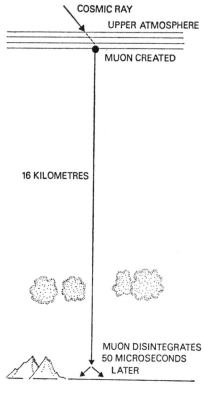

MUON'S VIEWPOINT

A high-speed muon is created at the top of the atmosphere and travels to the ground, where it disintegrates. From the earth's viewpoint it falls 16 kilometres and, by Einstein's time dilatation, lives for 50 microseconds. From the muon's viewpoint, it lives for 2 microseconds only (its 'proper' lifetime) but, by the Fitzgerald-Lorentz length contraction, the atmosphere seems to be only 0.6 kilometres thick.

about 16 km. up, by incoming radiations from space. These muons then come hurtling down, almost at the speed of light, and many of them get to ground level before they break up, and so must live for about 50 microseconds at these high speeds.

We can use this real effect to discuss another aspect of relativity. Suppose that we were riding in, through the atmosphere, on the back of one of these muons. We would know that the atmosphere was rushing past us at a relative speed nearly equal to that of light. We would also have our own clock, the 2 microsecond lifetime of our muon, at rest relative to us. We would thus come to the view, that by our reckoning the atmosphere is only 0.6 km. thick! This effect, which is of course quite general, is the *Fitzgerald–Lorentz contraction*: the length of a moving body, in its direction of motion, appears contracted. As with time dilatation, the effect is extremely small at 'ordinary' speeds and only becomes large at speeds approaching that of light.

The Time Machine

There is a symmetry between what we on the ground see of the man in the plane and what he sees of us. We see life in the plane being lived slowly and he sees just the same of us. But there is a way to produce an extraordinary asymmetry out of this. Einstein's theory led to the famous 'twin paradox' that, if one of two twins goes off on a wild, high-speed, there-and-back tour of the universe, he will find when he gets back that he has aged *less* than his stay-at-home twin.

People have tried hard to escape the iron logic of this spectacular aspect of Einstein's theory. Why, for example, can we not think of the second twin as moving, instead, and the first as standing still all the time? For this we would simply have to let the first twin take a pre-Copernican attitude and regard himself as at rest in a universe in which everything else was moving. By Einstein's argument, he would then be the *older* twin, when they meet again, and since he cannot be both younger and older the theory must be wrong!

To deal with this, think of two twins, each with a clock and flashlight, moving apart at uniform speed. Each flashes signals, at one-second intervals by his own clock, to the other. Because the distance between them is increasing all the time however, each signal has farther to go than its predecessor and so takes longer to make the journey. Thus, each twin deduces, from the signals coming in, that the other's clock is apparently running slow. This effect, which is *different* from time-dilatation (although there is also a little

Once a second, by his own clock, each twin flashes a time signal to the other. During Act 1 they move apart and, as a result, each one's clock seems to the other to be going slowly.

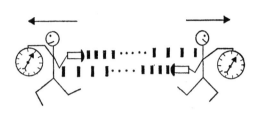

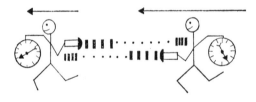

The left twin keeps his motion constant during all three acts. But in Act 2 the right twin has reversed and is chasing the left twin at extra high speed. Because he is now running to meet left's signals, as they come towards him, these signals give him the impression that left's clock is going faster.

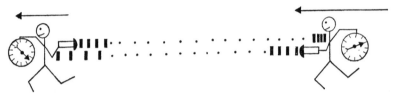

In Act 3 the news of right's turn around has reached the left twin. Each is now seeing the other's clock go fast.

When they meet, at the end of Act 3, the right twin has aged less than the left one, because, during Act 2, his clock was running slowly according to left, and left's clock was running fast according to him.

of that in it as well, at high speeds) is a form of 'red shift' or Doppler effect.

Eventually, one of the twins turns round and heads back at extra speed towards the other (who continues with unchanged motion), so that they now close at the same relative speed as they were previously separating. This leads to a corresponding apparent speeding-up of each other's clock, or 'blue shift'.

We can divide this whole play into three acts. The first act is when each sees the other's clock running slow, equally so for both, by symmetry. The second act opens when the one twin turns round and speeds back. He *immediately* sees the other's clock speeded-up; but throughout the second act the news of his turn-around has not yet reached the other twin, who continues to see his clock as slowed-down. The third act begins when the news of the turn-around reaches the other twin, who then sees the distant clock change from red shift to blue shift. Thereafter, all is symmetrical again. Each sees the other's clock equally speeded up.

Taking the play as a whole, there is a lack of symmetry in the happenings. The turn-around twin sees the other's clock red-shifted for one act and blue-shifted for two. The other twin sees the turn-around's clock red-shifted for two acts and blue-shifted for only the final one. At the end of the drama, the turn-around twin has thus aged less than the other.

A *time machine* is thus scientifically possible, although it can only take us forwards in time. The effect could be spectacular. Bondi has pointed out that we could, for example, make a 40-year journey, by our reckoning, out into space and back, in four equal stages: speeding up out, slowing down out, speeding up back, and finally slowing down back, at all times changing speed only at the rate at which we fall in the earth's gravity, so as to feel quite comfortable. But in doing this, we would have travelled 24,000 light-years from earth, and when we got back, 40 years older by our reckoning, we would find the earth over 48,000 years older than when we left! Space travel to very distant places, and time travel into the far future, are thus not at all difficult, biologically. The technical problem of providing rockets to do this is another matter, of course.

3

The Law of the Universe

Free Fall

Galileo climbed the leaning tower of Pisa and opened his hand, letting go a light ball and a heavy one. They struck the ground together and philosophers were amazed. A fable perhaps: but Galileo did prove that all bodies fall equally (except for air resistance) and so overturned the conventional wisdom of the time. Gradually, however, it got taken for granted as something useful in calculations of orbits and trajectories, and merely that. Only centuries later, did Einstein realise its tremendous significance.

But there were other aspects to gravitation, e.g. things that fall farthest, fall hardest. Galileo sharpened this familiar fact into the discovery that things fall to earth with *constant acceleration*. In the last chapter we met *constant velocity*, in which doubling the time doubles the distance moved. In constant acceleration, starting from rest, doubling the time doubles the *velocity*, so that the distance moved is quadrupled; i.e. the distance increases as the *square* of the time. A free-falling object on earth in one second of fall increases its speed by nearly 10 metres per second (neglecting air resistance). In other words, its acceleration is nearly 10 metres per second per second. For example, starting from rest, it falls about 5 metres in the first second, since its *average* speed during this first second of acceleration is some 5 metres per second.

Newton took the first step towards a universal law. His

brilliant idea was that the moon's orbit and the apple's fall are really the same, both due to the earth's gravity. A cork fired horizontally from a child's pop-gun drops to the ground a few metres ahead; a good archery shot goes much farther and a high-velocity bullet farther still. Newton imagined a bullet fired horizontally, above the atmosphere, with immense speed to take it hundreds or thousands of kilometres forwards. So far in fact that the earth's curvature comes into play. As the bullet drops towards the ground, so the ground curves away from it due to the great distances travelled. In fact, when it goes at about 8 kilometres a second, the dropping and curving exactly balance. It is then always accelerating towards the earth, without getting any nearer! It is in orbit, just like the moon.

Newton imagined a cannon on a high mountain, above the atmosphere, firing shots at ever higher speeds, so that they fall farther and farther away, until eventually one goes fast enough to circle the earth at constant height and so become a satellite.

There is a difference, however. Galileo's particular value for the acceleration is valid only near the earth. Newton recognised, from the orbits of the planets, that the gravitational influence of a body such as the sun is weaker at large distances. His famous 'inverse square' law of gravitation expressed this precisely: at twice the distance the acceleration is only one-quarter as much; i.e. the acceleration 'falls off' as the *square* of the distance. Newton knew that the moon is 60 earth-radii away; and so, knowing also that the distance of fall increases as the square of the time, he deduced that the moon should take 1 minute to fall as far as an apple on

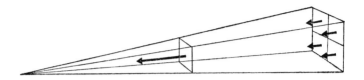

The inverse-square law. At twice the distance, from the centre of gravitation, there are four times as many unit squares over which the gravitational field is spread. Hence the gravitational effect there is only one quarter as strong.

earth falls in 1 second. It does! It is deflected towards the earth, away from a straight-line path, by about 5 metres in 1 minute.

The great testing ground for Newtonian gravitation was the solar system. The planets obeyed his law so perfectly in their orbits that it was even possible to predict, from their motions, the existence and exact positions of the two outermost planets, Neptune and Pluto, before they were discovered by astronomers. Although extremely simple, the law is not easy to use in such problems because everything influences everything else gravitationally – the apple also affects the earth – and sorting out all the planetary influences on one another's motions is a complicated exercise in celestial mechanics.

Because the strength and the direction of the acceleration both depend upon where one is, in relation to a centre of gravitation, the influence of that centre is said to be *inhomogeneous*. Our tides, caused by the moon's influence, show this. In the open seas there are two tides per 24 hours. On the side where the earth faces the moon, the water there is nearest to the moon and so is pulled towards it most and heaped up into a tide. But equally, on the opposite side the water is farthest away from the moon and so, being pulled towards it least, is 'left behind' by the earth accelerating towards the moon, and heaped up once more to make a second tide.

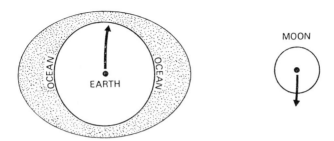

The moon produces two high tides on opposite sides of the earth. The water on the side near the moon is strongly pulled towards it, by its gravitational field, and so is heaped up there. The water on the far side is pulled towards the moon less strongly than the earth as a whole is pulled and so moves farther away, thus heaping up into a second high tide on that far side.

Newton's law takes us from the apple to the moon and thence to the sun and planets. Does it hold throughout the universe? Certainly it has been found to govern the rotations of close stars round each other (*double stars*) and to accord with the general structures of clusters of stars and galaxies. But the universality is contained in the 'inverse square' itself. If the earth were a perfect sphere its gravitational influence would be exactly symmetrical and would have the same strength at every place on a spherical surface centred on it. The *total* influence, over the whole of that surface, is exactly the same at each such surface, whether big or small. If we visualise this total influence as something 'coming' from the earth, it is completely *conserved* from one surface to the next, going outwards; none is lost, or gained. But the area of a spherical surface increases as the square of its radius and, since the total influence to be spread over the area is always the same, it has to be spread so much more thinly over the bigger surfaces, i.e. *inversely* as the square of the radius. But nevertheless, being conserved from one surface to the next, it reaches out into the depths of space. Newton's apple affects the stars in their courses.

Principle of Equivalence

But what is gravitation? Einstein's extraordinary answer, which he deduced from Galileo's discovery, was that it is an aspect of the structure of space-time. Let us repeat Galileo's experiment, but inside a spaceship. When this is out in space and coasting freely, with its rockets switched off, we let go the light and heavy balls. They now simply sit at rest, floating in the cabin alongside our opened hand. We now repeat the experiment but this time with the rockets on, so that the ship is accelerating. We see them 'fall' to the floor. Moreover, they fall exactly together since, from their point of view, they are still floating freely in space and it is *we* who are accelerating, past both of them. Now for Einstein's key point. Because they fall exactly together, we could not tell whether their motion, as we see it, is caused by our acceleration or by the pull of some big gravitational body, behind the ship. In other words, because all things fall equally, *acceleration is equivalent to gravity*.

This is Einstein's principle of equivalence and it opens up a marvellous way to study gravity by turning it into geometry (or, strictly, into *kinematics*, the geometry of space and time). For example, suppose that our spaceship is standing still on earth, with its rockets switched off, and that we send a flash of light from a lamp on the floor to a receiver on the ceiling. We can use Einstein's principle to turn this situation into the equivalent one in which the ship is out in space, far away from all gravitational centres, with its rockets accelerating it at 10 metres per second per second. This is now a purely kinematic problem. During the time that the light is climbing from the floor to the ceiling, the ship is gathering speed and the light has to chase a ceiling which is running away, increasingly fast, from it. Hence there is a velocity of separation between the floor, as it was when the light started off, and the ceiling as it is when the light gets there.

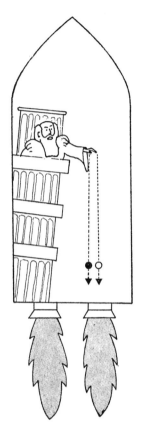

If Galileo had performed his experiment in a rocket, in outer space away from all gravitational bodies, which is accelerated by the thrust of its motors, he would have obtained the same result, because acceleration is equivalent to gravity.

As we saw in the last chapter, this is just the situation that leads to the Doppler effect. The frequency of the light received at the ceiling is lower than was sent out from the floor; i.e. there is a red shift from the floor to the ceiling (and a blue shift the other way) due to the acceleration. Similarly, if we send the light in pulses, at one a second according to a clock on the floor, they will arrive at slightly longer than one-second intervals, according to a clock on the ceiling. Time on the floor of the accelerating ship thus runs slower than time on the ceiling! Ordinarily of course, the difference is very small. For the above acceleration and a ceiling 3 metres high, it is about 1 second in 100 million years!

We now reverse the whole argument, by switching off the rockets and standing the ship on earth. The effects we have been describing must then be exactly the same, since we are replacing the acceleration from the rockets by the equivalent gravitation from the earth. And so we arrive at Einstein's *gravitational red shift*: light is reddened when it climbs against gravity; and clocks run slower near gravitational bodies. The measurement of this red shift has proved difficult, but good evidence was obtained a few years ago from the spectrum of a white dwarf star. A spectacular verification has also been obtained on earth by dropping pulses of gamma rays from a 25-metre tower to the ground. This depended on something called the *Mossbauer effect*, which enables these rays to be made and measured with extraordinary precision in frequency.

Downfall of the Straight Line

Galileo's discovery inspired Einstein still further. If the space-time paths of free-falling bodies are all the same, irrespective of how much material there is in those bodies or of what kind it is, then perhaps those paths are *features of space-time itself*. This seems a fantastic interpretation of Galileo. How are we to view it? As invisible tramlines guiding the bodies round curves when their inclination is to go straight on? No; we must think of empty space as empty, and that means that near gravitational bodies it is *curves*, not straight lines, that are the *natural* paths of free bodies. Newton said that a moving body would continue with constant velocity if left to itself. In other words, its track in space-time would be a straight line. We have grown so used to this idea that we never feel the need for invisible tramlines to keep it on *this* particular type of path. But what is so special about the straight line, in a world of spherical stars, orbiting planets and spiral galaxies?

Even the geometry of the earth's surface, on which we

live, is not 'straight line' geometry but that of a roughly spherical surface. Of course, from our three-dimensional point of view we can easily visualise and grasp the idea of the curved two-dimensional 'space' of the earth's surface. But we are embedded inside four-dimensional space-time and cannot 'get outside' this to look at its curvature. The idea of curved space-time thus remains difficult. When told that the natural space-time path between two given points is a curve, we inevitably wonder why we cannot by-pass this curve and cut directly through, in a straight line, from one point to the other. Very well, let us try to do this. Obviously it is no use shooting bullets or anything like that, in the hope of tracing a straight path, since it is their curved flight that is the basis of our problem. But there are still two other possibilities: to use a beam of light; or to apply a geometric principle, e.g. that the 'straight line is the shortest distance between two points'.

The first possibility fails, because gravity bends light. This comes directly from the finite speed of light. Suppose that a lift is falling freely down its shaft. Inside, no gravitational influence is felt and the straight line reigns supreme. Let a flash of light go horizontally, straight across the lift, as seen by someone inside. But to us, standing on earth outside the shaft and watching the lift hurtle down past us, the flash is seen to deflect towards the earth as it flies across; for we see it keep level with everything else inside the lift, all of which moves down together during its transit. Standing at rest and experiencing the earth's gravity, we thus conclude that *light itself also falls*. Einstein showed that this gravitational deflection of light should cause the positions of stars to appear to be shifted slightly when their light passes close to the sun. Testing this has been an exciting challenge, particularly during eclipses of the sun when such stars become visible, but good evidence has come recently through the sun's deflection of radio waves from very remote objects.

Light, then, also gives us curved space-time. Note that it

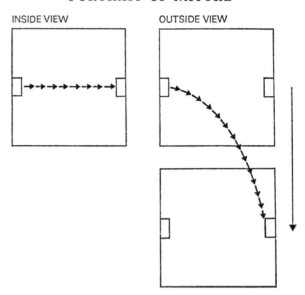

Inside a box where there is no gravitational field a beam of light shines straight across from the middle of one wall to the middle of the opposite wall.

There is no gravity inside the box because the box is falling freely in a gravitational field. To someone at rest in the field, outside the box, the light appears bent because the box falls while the light is going across it (shown greatly exaggerated). Hence light falls in a gravitational field.

is *space-time*, not just space, that is curved. A flash of light flies much straighter in space than, say, an arrow, because its flight is so brief. The arrow may go only 100 metres through space, but in space-time its journey is enormous because one second of time is equivalent to 300,000 km. of space; its slight arching over this long space-time path produces a big swerve in space, rather as a slightly bent rod looks strongly warped when viewed endways on.

But when we talk of curved space-time, do we not need the straight line, after all, as a standard of reference against which to judge the curvature? In elementary geometry, the straight line is the shortest distance between two given points. Can we not use the same idea in space-time? In

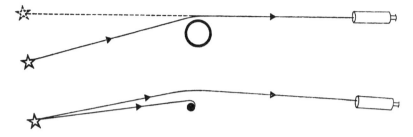

Starlight is deflected as it passes close to another star, on its way to the observer. But if that star shrinks down to become a black hole, light which grazes it closely is pulled right in by the tremendous gravitational field. In the same way, no light can escape from a black hole.

fact this is exactly what is done – apart from a technicality due to the fact that space-time is not space – but the lines it gives are *curved* near gravitational bodies. By analogy with the corresponding lines of least distance between distant points on the earth's surface, these lines in space-time are called *geodesics*. In space-time the problem is to find the line between two events, e.g. the event of an arrow leaving the bow and the event of its striking the butt. The geodesic, for free fall between these two events, is the line along which a travelling clock marks out *most time* (the change from least distance to most time is the technicality mentioned above). Newton's straight line is a geodesic when there is no gravitational influence.

This geometry of space-time was developed by Einstein into his *General Theory of Relativity*, the intellectual grandeur of which is fully worthy of a law of the universe. His equations take into account the fact that the gravitational influences of real bodies are inhomogeneous, as we saw when discussing tides. The complete theory is magnificently general. It deals with light as well as matter. In small regions of space-time it gives all the results of the special theory of relativity again, but it also deals with the largest regions and has opened up an entirely new picture of the universe. Where

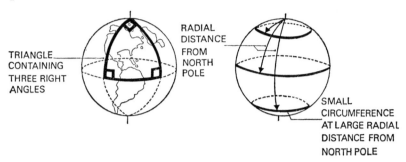

TRIANGLE CONTAINING THREE RIGHT ANGLES

RADIAL DISTANCE FROM NORTH POLE

SMALL CIRCUMFERENCE AT LARGE RADIAL DISTANCE FROM NORTH POLE

The earth's surface is an example of a *two-dimensional curved space* which we ordinarily think of as a curved surface belonging to a familiar 'straight' three-dimensional space. But, considered in itself, it shows some real and typical features of curved space. For example, the angles of a large triangle on it add up to more than two right angles; and the circumference of circles, drawn round it at various radial distances from the North Pole, do not increase proportionately to this radial distance. They even decrease to zero as the South Pole is approached. Curved space-time should be thought of as a four-dimensional arena of geometrical effects similar to these.

gravity is weak it gives Newton's law of gravitation again, but it also gives slightly different planetary motions which have been verified in the case of Mercury; and where gravity is strong or is changing rapidly it predicts remarkable new effects.

Spheres of Influence

How are we to imagine an actual piece of curved space-time; for example that which gives the earth's gravitation, as described by Newton's law? For this, let us go back again to the *space* picture of the family of spherical surfaces with a common centre, because of their usefulness for visualising the symmetrical gravitation round such bodies. We wander all over and through these surfaces, with rulers and clocks, making measurements. If we attach clocks to the surfaces – or in other words fix clocks at various distances from the common gravitational centre – then the clocks near the centre go slower than the others, as we have already seen. This clock effect already brings in what is, from the everyday point of view, the most important feature of curved space-time, i.e. the Newtonian gravitation to which it is linked by the principle of equivalence.

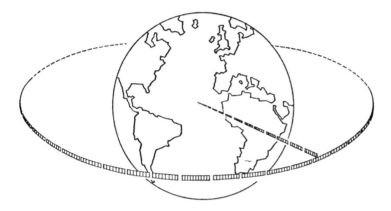

A girdle of rulers encircles the earth. The number of rulers in the girdle gives its circumference as twice that of the earth. But a line of the same rulers, down a radius to the surface of the earth, shows its radius to be (very slightly) more than twice that of the earth. This deviation from elementary geometry is an effect of the curvature of space round a spherical gravitational mass.

Crawling over any spherical surface with our rulers, we would discover an ordinary familiar geometry, and could measure its area by charting it with a network of small rulers. Similarly for all the others. Pointing our rulers now towards the centre, we could next measure the distance between two such charted surfaces. We would at this stage find something different from elementary geometry. This distance would *disagree* slightly with the rule, from elementary geometry, that areas of spherical surfaces are as the squares of their radii. One way of visualising this effect is to think of our rulers as *contracted* when pointed at the centre, more strongly so the closer they are; so that as we move towards the centre, from one surface to the next, the distances between these surfaces seem to stretch out as our rulers get shorter.

This, with the clock effect, completes our picture of symmetrical curved space-time round a gravitational centre. Almost, that is, because we still have to put *size* into it. As described so far, the same picture applies equally well, whether the centre is the sun, earth, moon, apple, or hydrogen atom. We need something that will put their similar geometries on to different scales, so that what happens at many millions of kilometres from the sun equally happens at a few kilometres from the moon and at the appropriate microscopic distance from the centre of the hydrogen atom. We need a characteristic radius, whose value for any particular centre indicates the spherical surface on which its gravitation has some standard value. The one used is the *Schwarzchild radius*, at which gravitational effects reach a certain limiting intensity which we shall discuss below. It is about 3 km. for the sun and 1 cm. for the earth. The smallness of these values is not surprising when we think of the weakness of gravity here on earth, over 6000 km. from the centre. We feel heavily weighed down by the earth's gravity, of course, but that is a subjective reaction; its effects on clocks and the bending of light are almost zero.

Let us forget about the real sizes of bodies for the moment and suppose that our concentric spheres go all the way in to a point centre. We then have a total picture of every such symmetrical region of curved space-time, typified by its value of the Schwarzchild radius. This picture even includes 'straight' space-time, which is simply the special case where the Schwarzchild radius is zero. What we find then, about our universe, is that these symmetrical curved regions exist in great abundance, at various strengths, as its most common feature. They make up the real space of the universe.

As we move towards the centre of one of these regions we find that the space-time curvature gets sharper – i.e. the gravitation gets stronger – and this continues, more and more severely, the closer we get. We are heading towards the heart of things, towards a 'singularity' where the effects run to wild extremes and where something drastically different from space-time as we know it must eventually appear. What do we find, in fact? Matter! This is perhaps the most fundamental way of considering the existence of matter in the universe – as the new aspect of nature which must appear where the space-time curvature runs away locally towards infinite sharpness.

But, what is the relation of matter to the Schwarzchild radius? First, an obvious point. Since this radius fixes the strength of the gravitational influences, we can use it as a measure of the 'amount' of matter present. But what about the physical size of this matter? In all the familiar examples this is vastly bigger than the Schwarzchild radius. The body in fact is 'inflated' by various non-gravitational effects which occur between its particles. On earth this inflation of a 1 cm. gravitational radius to a physical body of over 6000 km. radius produces an overall density of about five times that of water. The sun and similar stars are inflated to still lower densities by the intense radiation bursting out through them from inside.

The particles of such a body are nevertheless all under one another's attractive gravitational influences and so try to move together. What happens when the radiation and other effects are no longer sufficient to hold them apart? When a star begins to run short of nuclear fuel its life becomes complicated – phases of both contraction and expansion occur; in certain cases there may be a great explosion, giving a *supernova* – but in the long run the gravitational influence wins and the old star shrinks down to a tiny fraction of its previous volume. A star such as the sun ends up as a white dwarf, about a million times as dense as water. But if the amount of matter is a little greater than that of the sun, the contraction does not stop at this stage. The star collapses further, to a *neutron star*, with all of its matter squeezed into a radius of about 10 kilometres, a thousand million times more dense even than a white dwarf. It is now fairly certain that rapidly rotating neutron stars have been observed, as the *pulsars* first discovered in 1968 by radio-astronomers.

If the amount of matter is slightly larger still, about twice that of the sun, the collapse does not stop even at this stage. In fact there is no known effect that can resist gravitation in this case, and the star should collapse right down into *inside* its own Schwarzchild radius and so become a *black hole*. This simple but ominous name is a fair description of one of nature's most remarkable objects. It is a hole because nothing inside it or which falls into it can escape; it is black because this inability to escape applies even to its light. In these days of space travel the idea of the 'escape velocity' – the least velocity an object needs, to escape completely away from a gravitational body – is familiar. The nearer the object is to the centre when it sets off, the greater is this necessary starting velocity. At the Schwarzchild radius it equals the velocity of light, so that even light cannot escape. Another way of looking at this is in terms of the gravitational red shift of light climbing away from such a body. This becomes more and more marked the nearer the source of light is to the centre; and light 'coming' from the Schwarz-child radius is totally 'reddened' to complete darkness. Time is also affected, as we would expect from its close relation with red shifts. The collapsing of a star to its Schwarzchild radius would appear to be dragged out interminably in its final stages, as seen by viewers outside, who would conclude that time itself comes to a halt at the Schwarzchild radius. The very place for the Mad Hatter's tea-party!

Although black holes cannot be seen, their gravitational influence should be felt outside them. In fact one or two curious double stars have been detected in which a visible member of the pair is found to be greatly influenced by an invisible and tiny but massive, companion which, in at least some cases, is strongly suspected to be a black hole.

In the Beginning

The cosmological red-shift shows us that the universe is expanding. Did it then start as a 'point', in the Beginning, which exploded as a 'big bang'? This is the most obvious interpretation of the expansion, but there are others. Perhaps the most famous rival is the *steady-state theory*. According to this we shall not be left with an empty universe when all the presently visible galaxies have moved away, because it is assumed that nuclei of matter are spontaneously and continuously created in the void, by an unknown process, and then come together to make new galaxies much like the existing ones, so that the universe in the large should look much the same at all times.

The facts, however, as well as the simplest solutions of Einstein's equations for a universe which seems to be much the same everywhere and in all directions, point strongly to a big bang. Several quite different ways of gauging the 'age' of the universe point consistently back to a unique time of several thousand million years ago; and if we imagine the expanding universe running backwards at its present rate then this is just the right amount of time to bring them all together, into an incredibly compact and hot 'singularity'.

There is other evidence. The sky is not totally 'dark', even after discounting all the starlight. There is also a background radiation, with wavelengths in the microwave radar range, a few centimetres long. It is extremely uniform all over the sky, which again shows that the universe is much the same in all directions, and its mixture of wavelengths is just what would be expected of heat radiation. It was in fact predicted, before its discovery, as a relic of the big bang, the exploding fireball of incredibly hot radiation and hydrogen. As the universe expanded, it cooled – because its radiation became 'stretched out' in both wavelength and intensity over larger regions of space – and galaxies condensed out of the hot gas. Some of the original radiation in that fireball has however managed to survive to this day, through the entire lifetime of the universe. Having experienced the full expansion of space, from the primordial singularity out to today's vast reaches, its waves have been enormously stretched out, like an expanded concertina, from their original extremely short lengths to today's microwave radar values. It is an awesome thought that we can still 'see' the firelight of the Beginning – but not totally surprising since modern telescopes readily detect galaxies whose radiation has been on its way towards us for much of the lifetime of the universe.

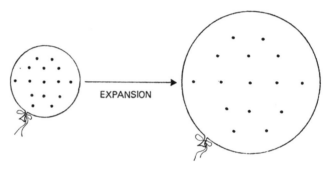

The expansion of the universe may be compared with the blowing up of a balloon, all the dots ('galaxies') of which move uniformly away from one another. Notice that the dots, above, do not themselves get larger; in the expansion of the universe it is the distance between the galaxies, not the galaxies themselves, that grows larger.

But what do we mean by 'the universe', when it is expanding? In general we mean the *visible* universe; ideally visible, that is, out as far as those regions moving away from us at the speed of light. This may be all there is, however, because the universe may be a *closed* world. Einstein showed from his general theory that, if a universe is of more than a certain density and size, matter and light could not escape from it, rather as they cannot escape from inside a Schwarzchild radius. We have seen that light is bent by gravity. Going through the universe it will be curved, in accordance with the curvature of space-time, due to the gravitational influence of all the matter in the universe; and if it goes far enough onwards in the same direction, through a closed universe, it will eventually come back to its starting point from behind. This is just like sailing round the world – also a closed 'space'.

It is possible that the universe is closed, although the evidence is not yet firm. Estimates based on all the visible contents of the universe give an average density about one-tenth of the required value for closure, which is roughly equivalent to one hydrogen atom per cubic metre. But there is also much invisible matter in the universe, such as inter-galactic hydrogen gas, cold stars and perhaps black holes, which could make up the difference.

The ultimate fate of the universe is closely bound up with this. The simplest universal solutions of Einstein's equations give two evolutions from a big bang: either an open universe which eternally expands; or, if the density is high enough for closure, a universe which expands to a maximum and then falls back again through its own gravitational influence – as a ball thrown in the air rises at first and then falls – to collapse into a second fireball singularity.

We cannot quite say yet, then, what our fate will be. Whether the universe will expand for ever, with more and more galaxies drifting away beyond our view, leaving us alone with the Milky Way. Or whether everything will come together again, thousands of millions of years hence, into a second fireball. And if this, whether it will explode to produce yet another universe, born out of the incineration of our own – as ours may have been from a predecessor.

4

Substance and Power

Forced Off Course

Why was Galileo's experiment amazing? Because the earth's gravity so obviously pulls harder on a cannon ball than a football, as our complaining muscles tell when supporting them. Since the same gravity acts on both, the strength of this *force* depends on something belonging to each such body itself, something which responds to this gravity more strongly in the cannon ball than the other. We measure it, of course, by *weighing* on scales or a spring balance. Weighing is basically the judging of this force against that on a standard amount of a reference substance, such as the litre of pure water (at 4° Centigrade) which is declared one *kilogramme*.

This is a second gravitational property of matter; not the active gravity of Chapter 3, but a passive property which is 'acted on' and which gives the force when its body is not allowed to fall. They are related. Suppose that a heavy ball is supported at the top of, say, a straight telegraph pole. This pole is a kind of elastic spring, compressed by a force all along its length. Looked at in the usual way, this force of compression resists the weight of the ball in the earth's active gravity. Looked at back to front, this force resists the weight of the *earth* in the ball's active gravity. Since it is the *same* force in both cases, the passive gravity of a body is proportional to the active gravity. They are made equal by choosing suitable units. Thus, instead of the Schwarzchild radius it is usual to use 'kilogrammes' or something similar.

A heavy ball is supported against gravity by a vertical pole. The force of elastic compression in the pole opposes the force of attraction between the ball and the earth. This force of elastic compression is the same – and hence so also is the gravitational force – irrespective of whether we think of the ball pulled by the earth's gravity or of the earth pulled by the ball's gravity.

The earth is about 6 million million million million kilogrammes.

The principle of equivalence now takes us on to a third example of the same property. A body standing on earth is, in the eyes of a freely falling 'weightless' observer, *accelerating upwards*. We can thus reinterpret the gravitational weight of this body as a force of resistance which appears when the body is accelerated off a geodesic course. But we do not have to be near the earth to have geodesics! Out in space, away from all local gravitational influences, this same force of resistance appears whenever a body accelerates off a geodesic course, but in this case we speak of the force as *inertia* and call the property of the body, to which it is proportional, *mass*. Even on earth, by accelerating in a horizontal direction, we can bring this force into play without involving the earth's gravity, as when we are forced back into our seats by a sudden jerk forwards in a train or car, or pressed against the side as it rounds a bend at speed.

Mass is *the* general property of substance, whereas weight is only a parochial aspect of it, not even constant at different places on earth. Mass is a *conserved* property – subject to a qualification we shall meet later – which means that the mass of a body is the sum of the masses of its parts and remains constant so long as no substance is added to or taken from the body. It can thus be regarded as the 'amount of substance' in a body, although there is a more fundamental way of looking at it.

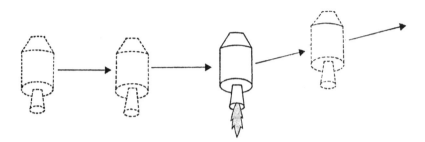

Conservation of momentum. A spacecraft coasting freely through space, well away from gravitational bodies, with its motor off, moves equally in equal times. With a short burst from its motor it then slightly alters its motion by ejecting a small mass at high speed in the opposite direction. The combined average motions of the craft and the ejected gas, when weighted in proportion with the two separating masses, equal the original motion.

For this, let us for simplicity work in a 'straight' spacetime, such as we have in and around a freely coasting spaceship which we can make our observational headquarters. On earth we would have to make do with a freely falling lift, or much more roughly, study the way things slide on a smooth frozen pond. In this space-time the straightness of the geodesics tells us that the motion of a free body is constant. With the passage of time the body neither gains nor loses velocity. Suppose however that, by purely internal action, the body splits into two pieces which spring apart and go their separate ways. Can we in some sense regard the body, taken as a whole, as conserving its previous motion? For this we have to find a way of averaging the motions of its two pieces, so that their new motions of separation cancel out in the addition, leaving the original motion extant as the only one representative of the body as a whole. Newton's first law of motion implies that there *must* be a way of doing this since the body as a whole, being at all times free of *external* influences, should continue on its way, as a whole, undisturbed. The fact that the two additional velocities of the pieces are in opposite directions makes a cancellation possible, since if we regard one as positive the other must then be negative. But we cannot simply average velocities; otherwise it would be possible for a flea, by jumping off a dog's back, to impel his astonished host with equal speed in the opposite direction. Instead we have to form a 'weighted average' in which each velocity is multiplied by some factor that represents its piece's share of the whole body. The inertial mass is just this weighting factor, which enables the total motion to be conserved. We thus arrive at the important *law of conservation of momentum* (i.e. mass times velocity) for a body in free motion. When such a body flies into pieces, the individual momenta of these add up – taking their directional properties into account – to give exactly the same overall momentum as before. This law is also true in curved space-time, provided the geometry of the curvature is taken into account when stating positions and times.

The All-Pervasive Universe

If weight is a parochial example of inertia, caused by the earth's gravity, what gravitational influence is responsible universally for inertia? It cannot be anything 'local', such as the sun or the Milky Way, because inertia is not exerted particularly in their direction. It must be the universe as a whole, through some total gravitational effect of all its substance, opposing any deviation of a body from geodesic courses which the universe lays down everywhere. Thus are we all affected by the ends of the universe! Everything is connected to everything else. One simple way of appreciating this is well known. Stand still on a starry night and notice that the stars are not visibly moving. Let your arms hang limply and pirouette round. You will feel them drawn outwards by centrifugal force, a form of inertia for rotary motion, at the same time as you see the whole sky of stars rotating. There is also Foucault's pendulum, a weight suspended from a long wire, free to swing in any direction, which ideally should be set up at the north or south pole. We start it swinging in a certain plane. It then goes on swinging in this same plane and ignores the rotation of the earth beneath it. To us, standing on earth, this plane moves round exactly in unison with the 24-hour rotation of the celestial sphere. We are thus brought to the view, put forward by Bishop Berkeley early in the 18th century and developed by Mach late in the 19th century, that inertial forces come from the matter of the universe as a whole and are brought into play when a body is accelerated relative to the universe.

But how does it work? It cannot be Newton's inverse square law, because this would make local objects, such as the sun, more influential than the distant ones, and inertia would then vary with the direction of acceleration. What in fact does the universe as a whole give us, irrespective of wherever we are? It gives a nearly straight space-time and also the 'universally' constant speed of light. There are several clues to suggest that inertia is connected with the speed of light. First, an argument based on dimensions. Inertia is a response to acceleration, which is distance moved 'per second per second'. At this fundamental level the only quantity we have that includes time is the speed of light, and this has to come in as the square, to give 'per second' squared. The rate of expansion of the universe also includes time, of course, but this may not be an independent quantity since, at the extreme distances from which most of the matter of the universe exerts its influence, the speed of expansion approaches that of light.

The 'twin paradox' discussed at the end of chapter 2 also suggests a connection. We explained the asymmetry there entirely in terms of the properties of light; the slower the speed of light, the longer it would take for the news of the one twin's turn-around to reach the other and so the greater would be the difference in age between them when they met. But the effect can also be explained in terms of inertia and gravitation. While he is turning round, the one twin is accelerating towards his brother and so is experiencing a force of inertia which can also be interpreted as equivalent to a gravitational influence – as if there were a 'source of gravity' behind him while he is reversing. Being nearer than his brother to this 'source', his clock runs slower during this period, with the result that he has aged less when he gets back. Calculations show that this gives exactly the same difference in ageing as we get from the purely optical argument, which strongly suggests a link between inertia and the speed of light.

How strong is the force of inertia? Another way of asking this question is – when a body falls freely under the earth's gravity, why does it accelerate only gradually, instead of dashing straight down at the speed of light? We are thus asking for a comparison of the earth's and the universe's gravitational effectiveness, at the earth's surface. On what do we expect this acceleration to depend? First, surely on the ratio of the earth's mass to that of the universe. And also on the square of the speed of light, so as to get in the 'per sec. per sec.' of acceleration. Again, because of Newton's inverse square law for the earth's gravity, we expect to have to divide by the square of the earth's radius. To get the dimensions of acceleration, we then need to multiply by one other length factor which, since we are considering inertia to be due to the most distant matter, must surely be the 'radius' of the universe. In fact, if we put all these contributors together, multiplied or divided in just this way, and then use values for the mass and radius of the universe as suggested by the astronomical observations outlined in chapters 2 and 3, the acceleration comes out roughly right.

Rotation

From this point of view, the free fall of the moon or a space satellite, orbiting round the earth, involves a balance between the earth's gravitational force and inertia due to acceleration towards the earth. There is a similar effect on the earth itself due to its spinning, although, since it takes 24 hours to go round, instead of the 90 minutes for a low-orbit satellite, the inertial force here is small compared with gravity. Small, but vital because it circulates the air over large areas of the planet and spreads the rainfall. It is seen most simply as a persistence of motion. Suppose for example that a wind is blowing northwards, off the equator. It starts off, carrying with it the full equatorial value of the earth's surface speed towards the *east*. As it gets into northern latitudes it passes over regions with smaller rotational speeds because there the earth's surface is nearer to its axis. The persistence of its original eastward equatorial velocity thus causes it to move eastwards as it blows north. And similarly, move westwards when it blows south again.

Due to this 'Coriolis effect', a large scale 'cyclonic' circulation of the air, north to east, south, and west, is thus set up; and a similar one rotating oppositely in the southern hemisphere. This is the pattern of the main wind movements on the earth. The wind tries to blow straight towards the 'depressions' – regions of low air pressure – but is caused instead to circulate round them, keeping almost to the 'isobars' of constant pressure and spiralling in only very gradually. As a result, depressions survive much longer than they would otherwise and so drift over great distances, carrying moist air from the oceans to inland places and making the earth more generally fertile.

There are many other examples of the Coriolis effect.

Rivers flowing north or south deflect towards the right – looking downstream – so that their right-hand banks are steeper than the left, in the northern hemisphere; and conversely in the southern one. Again, northern Europeans are blessed by the warm Gulf Stream, which turns eastwards as it flows northwards in the Atlantic.

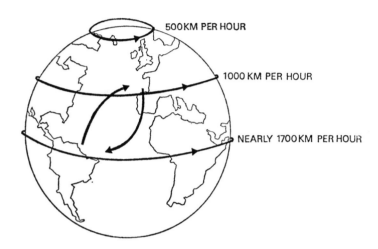

The speed of rotation of the earth's surface is greatest at the equator and least at the poles. Air or water which travels northwards from the equator thus has a greater sideways speed than the earth's surface in the northerly latitudes. As a result, this air or water turns to the east as it moves north. And similarly turns to the west when it moves south. This is an example of the *Coriolis effect*. The opposite motions occur in the southern hemisphere.

The persistence of motion in freely rotating bodies shows itself in many different ways and it is related to the fundamental law of *conservation of angular momentum*. Although in some ways similar to the *linear* momentum discussed earlier, angular momentum is more complicated because uniform rotation is a special kind of acceleration in which the direction of the velocity changes, but not the speed. The distance of a rotating body from the axis plays a crucial part. Those bodies far out from the axis may take a long time to circle round it – so that their 'angular velocity' is low – even though their local speeds on the circumference may be high. For example, the solar system is going at the – for us – tremendous speed of 250 km. per sec. but takes 250 million years to circle the galaxy. And so angular momentum depends on the distance out to the rotating body, as well as on its mass and its speed on the circumference. A figure skater uses this to bring her performance to a spectacular conclusion. She goes into a slow pirouette with her arms outstretched and then pulls them in, getting all of herself as close as possible to her axis of rotation, so as to bring about a dazzlingly fast spin.

The skater uses conservation of angular momentum to produce a fast spin.

Rotation is very common in the universe. If bodies, attracted to one another gravitationally, happen not to come together exactly along the line between centres – because of their initial motions when they were far apart – then their persistence of angular momentum will cause them to rotate rapidly round one another when they get close. Thus are the planets, stars and galaxies in various states of rotation. The sun turns on its own axis about once a month, but if it were to shrink to the size of a neutron star, conservation of angular momentum would require it then to spin at about 1000 turns a second.

Pulsars and perhaps also black holes are believed to owe many of their special properties to rapid rotation. Particles of interstellar gas, attracted into them, spiral round them and, through these fast rotations, generate intense radiations. The pulsar in the Crab Nebula, for example, is known to be pouring out 100,000 times as much radiation as the sun. At the centres of some galaxies there may be 'supermassive' objects, a million times the mass of the sun, made up of lots of pulsars or possibly consisting of a huge black hole surrounded by a rapidly rotating disc. The same kinds of processes would occur there on a titanic scale, as stars and other matter spiral into the inferno, giving such enormous outputs of radiation as to make them visible from the other side of the universe, as quasars and other extraordinary galactic objects.

The Currency of Nature

A body cannot increase its momentum by its own internal efforts. But this does not seem a great restriction since momentum, being a directional quantity, can be created in equal and opposite amounts – out of the blue, as it were – by the body splitting into pieces which spring apart. In a sense, motion is certainly created in this way. If we take the squares of the new velocities, to eliminate negative signs through the fact that two 'minuses' make a 'plus', we seem to have got something for nothing. Have we solved the problem of the perpetual motion machine? Alas no; for nature has economic rules as strict as any bank manager. And they are applied through the law of conservation of another property, this time a non-directional one.

It is *energy*. We all know of its importance. Newspapers proclaim energy crises as politicians clamour for energy policies. Advertisements tempt us with energy-giving breakfast foods and the dynamic man of tireless energy claims his admirers, although fewer than formerly. But what is energy? Its importance and elusiveness both come from the same thing; its chameleon-like nature. There are many different kinds of energy which change readily, one into another, but with the total always remaining the same. Energy is nature's convertible currency.

The simplest example of energy is mechanical *work*, which is what a force does when it moves, and it is equal to the force multiplied by the distance moved forwards along its line of application. This is work done *by* the force. By contrast, if the force is pushed backwards against its resistance – as when an elastic spring is compressed or a weight lifted – work is done *on* the force. The 'source' of the force is then said to have increased its *potential energy* by the amount of work done on it, so that your legs get tired, climbing a hill, by working to increase your gravitational potential energy. One of the oldest measures of energy, the *foot-pound*, in fact is defined simply as the work done in lifting 1 lb. by 1 ft. A man has the *power* to work at the rate of about 50 ft.lb. per sec. The picturesque unit based on what a good horse can do gives us the *horse-power*, 550 ft.lb. per sec.; but horses are giving way in this mechanical age to the *watt* and *kilo-watt* (i.e. 1000 watts, equal to $1\frac{1}{3}$ horse-power), and to the energy units, *joule* (1 watt working for 1 second) and *kilowatt-hour*.

Moving bodies also can do work, as when a train runs into buffers and compresses their springs, or a salmon leaps up a waterfall. They have energy of motion, or *kinetic energy*, equal to the square of the speed multiplied by half of the mass. A simple example of the interchange of kinetic and potential energy is seen in the pendulum. At the ends of its swing the suspended bob is momentarily at rest, with no kinetic energy but, being then also at its highest point, with greatest potential energy. As it drops back, gathering speed, it gains kinetic energy at the expense of potential energy, until it sweeps at maximum speed through the lowest point of its swing with greatest kinetic and least potential energy. Thereafter it climbs back to the highest point again, on the other side, by changing kinetic back into potential energy. Apart from some leaking away of energy, due to friction, the conservation of energy in these exchanges ensures that the potential energy is fully returned in each cycle.

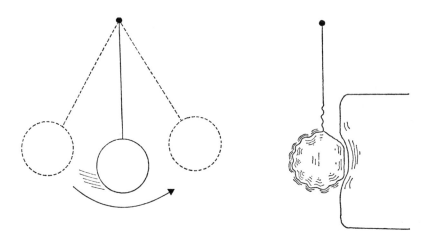

When a heavy lead pendulum is pulled up to one side and then allowed to swing, the gravitational energy released by its fall becomes kinetic energy of motion, as the pendulum sweeps at high speed through its lowest point. This motion is reversible: the pendulum climbs equally up the other side, converting its energy back to gravitational again, so continuing the swinging motion. If the pendulum crashes into a heavy body, however, its kinetic energy becomes disorganised and no longer capable of lifting it up any more. This is an irreversible process and the mechanical energy is turning into heat energy.

As well as these mechanical forms, energy can exist in many others. As for example when we use a 100-watt light bulb, which absorbs electrical energy at the rate of 100 watts to give us a mere 5 watts of light energy and all the rest as heat energy. The intense radiation which pours out of pulsars and similar objects shows the place of radiant energy in the law of conservation. Gravitational potential energy is converted into kinetic as the attracted matter spirals in and thence into radiation by electrical processes.

The fact that *heat* is a form of energy and must be included in the energy conservation law, which as a result changes its name to the *First Law of Thermodynamics*, was one of the great scientific findings of the 19th century. Heat is mechanical energy in a disorganised form. The particles of a pendulum bob all swinging together have an orderly motion, like a troop of men marching in formation, but if the bob crashes into something and starts shaking violently within itself, the motion of the particles becomes disorderly, as if the troop had broken up into a rabble of men moving randomly to and fro. *Friction*, due for example to two surfaces rubbing together and stimulating fine-scale motions in each other, is the familiar way in which mechanical energy is turned into heat. Thus, bringing a fast car to a screeching halt heats the brake drums appreciably.

Energy, like money, is measured in unnecessarily many currencies. The favourite ones for heat are the *calorie*, the heat to raise 1 gramme of water by 1° Centigrade, equivalent to about 4.2 joules, and the dietician's *Calorie* of food value, equal to 1000 calories. On average we eat some 2400 Calories in 24 hours, which is about a 100 watt energy rate.

Since it is so interconvertible, can we not get the same energy to work for us over and over again? Is this yet another way to perpetual motion? Again no, because when we use it some inevitably gets disorganised – friction turns mechanical energy into heat – which leaves us with the problem of trying to get work out of a lot of individual motions which are no longer co-ordinated. In place of a disciplined force we have a rabble. It follows that, although mechanical energy can easily be turned into heat – friction does just this – it is very difficult to go the other way. You can stop a car by making its brake drums hot, but you cannot then use this heat to drive it again. This *irreversibility* is the message of the

Second Law of Thermodynamics. If the first law says in effect that we cannot get something for nothing, the second says that we cannot break even, either!

The point is that in complex bodies there is an almost endless set of possible motions available for the energy, practically all of which are the higgledy-piggledy ones we call 'heat'. The orderly 'mechanical' motions, being so few, by comparison, are rare, so that once the energy flows out of a mechanical motion into the labyrinth of heat motions, the chance of it finding its way back again by blind action is negligible. A stone or stream of water will run down a hillside and eventually come to rest at the lowest level; it will not gather itself together again and roll back. The idea of mechanical *stability* in nature is closely related to this. Something with free mechanical energy is likely to change, because this energy can, through a force, cause spontaneous motion, which may continue until the lowest level of mechanical energy is reached, when the change can go no farther. After being run in from a tap above, the bath water gradually settles down to rest, unless externally disturbed.

It is difficult to go from heat to work, but not entirely impossible. A limited amount of mechanical energy can be got from heat, which is what steam and internal combustion engines and turbines do, and the possibility of this depends on the *temperature* of the heat. Our contact with hot water bottles or cold swimming pools tells us that heat flows from hot bodies to cold. In such a flow there is a bit of orderliness through the fact that the heat is all flowing in *one* direction; and we can take advantage of this, in clever mechanical devices which, in effect, place 'paddles' in the way of this flow, to be turned by it, so extracting some work from the heat. In a modern power station, about one-third of the heat energy from the fuel is converted into electrical energy. The higher the temperature at which the extraction is done, relative to the surroundings, the more efficient is the conversion. Temperature is a measure of the *intensity* of the

heat energy in a substance; a small amount of intensely concentrated heat gives a spark its incandescently high temperature; a large amount of sparsely distributed heat gives a
swimming bath its tepid temperature. Since heat is a form of
motion there is a lowest possible temperature. This is
absolute zero, roughly − 273° c.

The Roots of Power

Again, what is energy? Roughly speaking, kinetic energy is
a kind of 'momentum' along the time axis. We have seen
that linear momentum is a directional quantity which
expresses the rate at which mass is shifted in a given direction through space. It is thus a collection of three separate
values, one for each of the axes of three-dimensional space,
and there is a conservation law for each. But space-time is
four-dimensional. It is thus natural to expect also a fourth
value, one for the time axis, again with a conservation law.
This fourth one in fact is kinetic energy. Compared with
linear momentum however, it has to contain an additional
speed factor to allow for the change from length to time for
this fourth axis; and so kinetic energy goes as the square of
the speed.

But we really have to look at the question relativistically.
From our observation post we are watching a moving mass.
What can we measure 'along our time axis' that will tell us
something about its speed relative to us? This question takes
us back again to that aircraft of chapter 2. We measure how
much time passes on our clock, for each second lapsed on a
clock carried by the moving mass. In fact, if we multiply
the mass by this *ratio of times* – and also by the square of the
speed of light to get dimensions right – we have a proper
expression of the energy of the moving mass in terms of
measurements along our time axis.

Several remarkable things come out of this. First, if the
speed of the mass is near that of light, the ratio of times is

almost infinite. In other words the mass cannot be got up to the speed of light because it would need to have infinite energy for this. Second, when the speed is low the ratio of times simplifies in just the right way to turn the kinetic energy into the familiar form of half mass times speed squared. The third result is even more striking. When the speed drops to zero the energy does not vanish, because the ratio of times simply drops to 1 in this case. The *resting* mass is left with an energy equal to its mass times the speed of light squared. We have in fact reached Einstein's equation which tells us that energy and mass are the same thing measured in different units, with the square of the speed of light coming in as the factor which multiplies mass units to turn them into energy units. This has become the most awesome equation in science, for it is the root of nuclear power.

The square of the speed of light is an enormous proportionality factor, so that a mere speck of matter, by our standards, is equivalent to a lot of energy. For example, 1 gm. is equivalent to about 25 million kWh., enough to heat and light a large city for a day. In most of the ordinary processes of our daily lives, the energy transactions are so small in relation to the masses involved that, to all intents and purposes, we have separate conservation laws for mass and for energy. But in reality there is only one law, for both mass and energy in toto, through the agency of Einstein's equation. In processes at very high velocities, or nuclear processes, or movements in regions of intense gravitation, matter can be converted into energy in larger amounts. When a uranium nucleus undergoes fission, for example, about one-thousandth of its mass is turned into energy. In quasars, the material spiralling into the centre may convert nearly half of its mass into energy, so providing a material basis for their enormous outputs of radiation.

For masses moving at high speeds the ratio of times no longer leads to a simple expression for kinetic energy. We have a choice between using a velocity given by distance gone during unit time of the *moving* clock, together with a constant 'rest mass'; or an 'ordinary' velocity based on unit time of our *stationary* clock, together with a 'moving mass' equal to the rest mass multiplied by the ratio of times and which rises to infinity at the speed of light. The second of these is commonly used. Consider, for example, a high-speed bullet ploughing into a fixed block of wood. Because of time dilatation the bullet seems to us to be going not quite so extremely fast and so, if we were mistakenly to use both rest mass and ordinary velocity, we would not expect it to go in quite so far as it does. If we stick to ordinary velocity then we must account for the extra momentum by taking the moving mass to be greater than the rest mass.

The Life-Giving Flux

When Olbers pointed to the dark sky he indicated one of the most profound features of the universe. It is a world of *different* temperatures. At one extreme are the stars, made hot by the release of gravitational energy during their formation from interstellar gas, and kept hot by thermonuclear processes which occur at these high temperatures. At the other is space itself, kept cold by its cosmical expansion which stretches out the wavelengths of radiation, expanding hot 'blue' into cool 'red'. Space itself is thus a vast unfillable vessel for the radiation pouring out of the stars; and, so long as the universe expands and the stars burn nuclear fuel, the flux of radiant energy from the stars into space must continue unabated, their efforts to 'fill' space with hot radiation and so raise it to their temperature being always defeated by the cosmical red shift.

The planets, and the earth in particular, are in the middle of all this. There is some leaking of heat from the earth's hot centre to the surface, but this is trifling compared with what we receive by radiation from the sun. In essence we are maintained by the sun. We get its energy in high-temperature form, in round figures at about 1 kilowatt per square metre. One-third of this is directly reflected back into space, making us externally visible by 'earthlight' just as we see the moon and planets by their reflected sunlight. The rest is absorbed as heat by the air, land and seas, with some used to evaporate water and to drive the rain-making and oceanic current cycles. Sooner or later however all of it is radiated out into space again, because the constancy of the earth's temperature, maintained almost perfectly over millions of years, means that our incoming and outgoing energies are in almost exact balance so far as the *quantity* of energy is concerned.

But not in *quality*. The energy we absorb from the sun is typical of a very hot body. That which we send out is typical of our own modest temperature. And it is to this difference that we owe most of the good material things in life, including life itself. We have seen that when heat flows from a high temperature to a low there is some orderliness in this process which can be exploited to extract mechanical – and other forms of – energy; to do work; to move things about; to make intricate and complicated things.

Nature does this, spontaneously; admittedly with very low efficiency but the total energy fluxes are so large that the small net effect is a tremendous one by our standards. The winds, waves, rains and rivers are all natural engines, making mechanical energy, and also electrical energy in thunderstorms, out of this 'degradation' of the sun's energy from high-temperature to low-temperature heat; and, in moving matter about through this work, they create further low-temperature heat from the disordering of this mechanical energy. But nature has also used the opportunity to develop much more exotic ways of capturing order from this energy flux, through the evolution of *life*.

A small fraction of sunlight is captured by the leaves of plants, where it is stored as chemical energy, i.e. as energy intrinsic to certain substances which are the basic constructional materials and foodstuffs of the entire vegetable and animal kingdoms. Again, there is a rough equilibrium. Over a period of a year or so there is an almost exact balance between the amount of such material created by this process of *photosynthesis* and that destroyed by rotting of dead vegetation in air and water. But not quite exact. Sometimes the organic material gets buried before it decays and it may then be preserved in an only partially degraded form. In this way the great coal deposits have been built up during the past 300 million years, under sediments of mud and sand.

Sometimes, also, it gets *eaten* and makes its way up 'the food chain' from vegetation to the lower and higher animals, and eventually to man himself. Here the same principle is still at work; the digesting of partly ordered energy by a system designed to filter out the valuable ordered component and turn it into some even more highly organised and complex things, while rejecting the bulk in a less organised form. This process no longer stops at man himself. We now have industrial society, which can be thought of as a system for converting organised energy into complex goods and services, on the one hand, and waste heat on the other.

We see how everything is coupled to the expansion of the universe; the energy flows, the astrophysical and geological processes, the evolution of life, and the development of modern society. Even *time* itself is probably a manifestation of the same universal feature. The universe, at least within our range of experience, exists in a linear sequence of states which are distinguished from one another by the increasing distances between distant galaxies. In all the states to one side of any given one, the universe is smaller; in all those on the other side it is larger. The line is distinguished at one end by the evidence for a unique state, the 'big bang'. What happens at the other end – whether the line 'tapers' again to another unique state or whether it is open-ended, an infinity of larger and larger sizes, we do not know. The line, as we find it here and now, is being explored systematically by the universe in the sense that we never experience any irregularity in the order of the states, as judged by the scale of distances. We attach the words 'earlier' to the smaller states and 'later' to the larger ones, and so fix an 'arrow of cosmological time' pointing from the known unique state towards the expanded states of the unknown 'future'. Radiation in space is stretched out and red-shifted by this expansion, so bringing about the imbalance in the distribution of energy which makes the stars *sources* of radiant energy when viewed in the direction of the cosmological arrow. And so the energy flux from the stars is set up, and with it the thermodynamical arrow of time and all the consequential evolutionary processes; the geological and historical records; and the development of life in its various forms, including ourselves and our intuitive awareness of time, with our memories of the past and anticipations of the future.

5

Charge and Countercharge

Two Kinds of Matter

So far, matter has seemed pretty featureless stuff. From whence come all the rocks, waters, air, mineral earths, metals, and the infinite variety of plant and animal kingdoms? Or the richly individualistic properties, the hardness and softness, the runniness of water and stiffness of ice, the clarity of glass and silveriness of metals, the flammability of wood and inertness of stone, the colours of the painter's palette, the textures of the dressmaker's fabrics, the saltiness and sweetness of foods?

It all comes from the workings of an incredibly small number of basic elements and general principles, rather in the way that we produce great libraries of different books from the same few letters used over and over again in various combinations according to a few rules of composition. And, just as in language we find words are generally mixtures of two kinds of letters – vowels and consonants – so we find, as the first portent of the variety of nature, that matter is generally a mixture of two kinds, which we call *positively* and *negatively charged*, respectively. Just as vowels and consonants congregate together, in the individual words on a page, so the positive and negative kinds of matter congregate together in space. No one knows why two 'unlike' charges attract each other or why 'like' charges – two positives, or two negatives – repel. Calling them 'charges', or using the grander names 'electrostatic forces' or 'electromagnetic fields', should not blind us to this fact. It is one of the basic mysteries, something we know but cannot explain (although Dirac has very recently revived an earlier theory of Weyl's which explains it in terms of a supposed variation in space of the standard of length, analogous to the explanation of gravitation in terms of the curvature of space). Nevertheless, a great science has been founded on it, which explains a vast range of other things.

Because these two kinds of matter congregate together, ordinary bodies as we know them – a table, this book – generally contain balanced amounts of both and are said to be electrically *neutral* or uncharged. They have no excess of either charge. But it is not difficult to produce some separation of the charges. We do this ourselves when we take off a nylon shirt in dry weather, which then crackles and sticks to the wardrobe door; and we experience a small 'electric shock' when we touch a doorknob after walking across a synthetic fabric carpet. Nature does it on a grand scale in thunderstorms. The word electricity in fact comes from the Greek name for amber, *elektron*, because the ancients knew that certain substances such as amber, after rubbing with a dry cloth, attract scraps of straw or feathers. We are familiar today with many *insulating* substances such as glass and sealing wax that can similarly acquire a *static* charge by friction – in which some of the charged matter of one substance is literally rubbed off, on to the other – and called 'static' because on an insulator the charge stays where it is put.

Electricity is *not created* by this process. A small amount of negative charge is transferred from the one substance to the other, so leaving the 'donor' with a small surplus of positive charge and giving the 'receptor' an exactly balancing amount of negative charge. In fact, electrical charge is a strictly conserved quantity. The total – positive minus negative – in an isolated body remains always the same. If, somewhere within the body, the amount of positive charge is increased, then also somewhere in the body there always appears an exactly equal increase in the amount of negative. The law of conservation of charge is even stricter than that of mass. If a charged body is set in motion, then, so long as it remains electrically isolated, its charge stays exactly the same. Charge does not increase relativistically with speed; unlike mass, it is a truly *invariant* property of matter.

Charge is easily measured. We could, for example, take two ping-pong balls held side by side on two long silk threads from a nail, charge them both by stroking with a dry cloth, and measure how far they spring apart against the force of gravity pulling them down together. Various electrical instruments in effect do this, more precisely. Millikan gave a striking demonstration by blowing a fine mist of oil drops, which he had arranged to pick up electrical charges, into the space between two horizontal flat plates, i.e. 'electrodes', one above the other. The electrodes were charged so as to attract the drops upwards, against the pull of gravity; by varying the electrode charges it was then possible to make the drops move up or down, or stand still.

Electricity is one of nature's strongest forces. How would we show this? Find out how much charge we could scrape off one body on to another? This is what is done in *Wimshurst* and *van der Graaf* generators. But the difficulty is that the charge, sooner or later, finds its way back again, often in an electric spark. The alternative is not to aim at bigger charges on existing bodies, but at existing charges on smaller bodies. What happens when a body is cut up into smaller pieces? Do we eventually reach pure fragments of charge?

J. J. Thomson answered this by his discovery of the *electron*, the particle of negatively charged matter. He fixed two electrodes some distance apart inside a glass tube under high vacuum, to which charges could be passed via metal wires leading in from the outside, rather as in a modern fluorescent strip light. When they were charged very strongly, a 'discharge' of electricity took place through the space between them and caused the glass vessel to glow. By putting small screens in the tube near the negative electrode – the 'cathode' – it was proved from the shadows which they threw on the glass that the glow was due to something – 'cathode rays' – streaming away from this electrode. By bringing up electrically charged plates, and also magnets, the stream could be deflected systematically. This apparatus was of course the forebear of today's cathode-ray tubes, in television sets.

In this way, it became clear that the stream consisted of negatively charged particles, now called electrons. It also proved possible to measure their ratio of charge to mass, which by all ordinary standards turned out to be enormous. The electrical force between two electrons is 4, followed by 42 noughts, times as strong as the gravitational force between them! No wonder that the electrical force has such a firm grip on the structure of matter. But if it is so strong, why do we not feel its effect, rather than that of the relatively puny gravitational force, across the universe? It is because charge exists in the two opposite forms, which are normally present in exactly balancing amounts in all large pieces of matter, so that their effects cancel out at a distance. By contrast, gravitation always has the same sign. All particles of matter attract one another gravitationally, whatever their nature, so that their weak individual attractions add up to an immense total when considered on a universal scale.

By further experiments Thomson estimated the charge on an electron and so, already knowing the ratio of charge to mass, also deduced its mass. Later, Millikan, with his oil drop method, did it more precisely. Needless to say, the mass of the electron is minute; 1 gramme of electrons would contain 1, followed by 27 noughts, of these particles. Electrons, from wherever they come, are all the same. They all have the same negative charge and the same rest mass; and of course this mass increases relativistically in the same standard way when they are moved at speed.

What about the other kind of matter, positively charged?

Later experiments were able to separate this, in a rather similar way, into beams of what are called *positive ions*, which also turn out to be charged particles. But these come in various different forms. The unit of positive charge they carry is always the same, and exactly balances the electron charge. But many ions can have one, two, three . . . or more such unit charges. Moreover, the masses of the ions are quite different for different substances. The lightest of all is the hydrogen ion, with only one charge, but its mass is nevertheless nearly 2000 times larger than that of the electron. One consequence of this is that, since the universe consists mainly of hydrogen, the number of material particles in it must be something like 1 followed by 80 noughts.

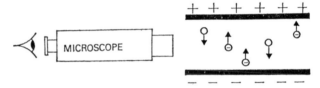

Millikan's oil-drop experiment. Fine oil drops were sprayed into the space between two horizontal metal plates. The oil drops were electrically charged by exposing them to ionising radiation and the metal plates were then increasingly charged, to attract charged oil drops upwards against the force of gravity. By balancing these two forces, so that some charged drops neither rose nor fell, as seen through the microscope, it was possible to determine the natural unit of electrical charge.

We compared, above, the strengths of the electrostatic and gravitational forces between electrons. This comparison makes sense because the electrostatic force also obeys the same 'inverse-square' law with distance, so that the ratio of the two forces is the same at all distances. In the electrical case, the law is known as *Coulomb's law*, and the force is given by the product of the two charges divided by the square of the distance between them. This is for empty space; the force can be different if there is other material about.

Here we have charge playing a part similar to gravitational mass and, when considering the electrical force acting on a particular body, we can think of the charge of this body playing a 'passive' role, being acted on by an electrical *field* of influence of the other charge playing an active role. This of course is simply a way of looking at things and, as with mass, the active and passive roles can be interchanged. Nevertheless, it is helpful to think of a centre of electrical charge in its active role as the *source* of a spherically symmetrical field of electrical influence, a field of invisible lines of force spread out through space round this source, lying in wait to act forcibly on any other charged particle that happens to come within range. The force on this particle, attractive or repulsive according to its own sign of charge, is then equal to the 'field strength' at the place where the particle is, multiplied by the value of its charge.

Currents of Charge

Early in the 18th century it was realised that metals conduct electricity. Differently charged bodies, however far apart, quickly send their charge from one to another when they are joined by a metal wire. We know today that this comes from a unique feature of the structure of metals – some of their electrons can move about freely inside them. A metal wire is thus like a channel holding a 'fluid' of electrons. Applying an electric field, by connecting its ends to differently charged bodies, is like tilting the channel, so that the charge of electrons runs down it, being replenished at one end from the source and pouring out of it at the other end.

Other things become conductors under special conditions. Pure water is a poor one but if a speck of salt or similar substance is dissolved in it, as for example in sea water, its conductivity is greatly enhanced. This is *electrolytic* conductivity, in which the moving charges are *ions*, for the great dissolving power of water for salty substances is due to its ability to shield their ions – both positive and negative ions, the latter having captured electrons from the former – from one another's Coulomb forces, so enabling them to escape and move as individual free particles throughout the liquid. In this case, when a field is applied, between two charged terminals or electrodes, there is a double flow of current, the positive ions swimming towards the negative terminal (cathode) and the negative ions towards the positive one (anode).

Insulators can be turned into conductors by various means. The *semi-conductors* familiar in transistor radios are insulating substances such as germanium and silicon which have been given a slight metal-like conductivity through the addition to them of certain 'impurity' substances. The earth's *atmosphere* is made slightly conducting at low altitudes by cosmic rays – high energy radiations from space – which occasionally collide with its molecules and knock electrons off them, so releasing charged particles; and also at very high altitudes, i.e. in the 'ionosphere', due to similar effects from the sun's radiation. At about 80 km., which is below the ionosphere, the air conducts well enough to act as a 'mirror' for short radio waves, enabling them to pass round the earth's surface by 'bouncing' back off it.

Heat, particularly at incandescent temperatures, can also turn things into conductors, by overcoming the electrical forces gripping the electrons to their positive ions, which can then escape as separate free charged particles. This happens particularly in hot flames. Ionised and conducting gases are called *plasmas*.

Finally, insulators can be 'broken down' into conductors through the sheer brute force of really strong electric fields. The most spectacular examples of this occur in the air, in electric sparks and lightning strokes. In a thunder cloud various updrafts and downdrafts of air occur, sweeping water drops and ice crystals with them, and a strong negative charge develops at the bottom of the cloud, with a corresponding positive one at the top. The strong electric fields between neighbouring clouds, or between the bottom of a cloud and the ground, may then be powerful enough to force conducting paths through the air and create giant arc discharges along them. Such a field can accelerate a free electron or ion to such high speeds, before it hits a molecule, that when it does hit one it knocks charged fragments off it, which then also accelerate and repeat the process, so that a 'cascade' or 'avalanche' of molecular break-downs occurs and a conducting path is cut through the material. A lightning stroke starts by forming a 'leader', which works its way down from the cloud in a series of steps, by the acceleration of electrons. When it does reach the ground it serves as a temporary conducting 'wire' connecting the cloud to the ground, along which the main stroke can then run. The huge electrical energy released by the rapid discharge of electrons, along this ionised channel, produces the brilliant flash; and the rapid expansion of the explosively heated air gives the thunderclap. Subsequent strokes may then take place along the same path. If there is a tall object on the ground nearby, such as a building with a pointed tip, the very strong electric field near this tip may set off a local discharge there, which goes out to meet the downcoming leader. The lightning stroke then preferentially strikes this tip. An external metal 'lightning conductor' from the tip to the ground is thus a useful feature, to protect a building from its damage.

Static electricity thus has its moments of glory, but electricity as we mainly know it today comes from quite different things, discovered in the years around 1800, which linked electricity first with chemistry and then later with magnetism. Galvani in the late 18th century, experimenting with the twitching of frogs' legs due to electric shocks, found that the same effect could be produced by the contact of two different metals, joined together. Volta followed this up systematically to show that pairs of different metals, such as copper and zinc in contact, acted like a 'pump' for electricity. By making a pile of such pairs, separated by paper pads soaked in brine or acid, in the order . . . copper, zinc, pad, copper, zinc, pad . . . etc., he greatly intensified the effect. The terminals at the ends of this pile performed like those from an electrostatic machine, except that a current of electricity could be drawn continuously from them and passed, through an external conducting circuit from one to the other, more or less indefinitely. He had made an electric *battery*, as in the modern dry cells and lead-acid accumulators.

The water electrolyte, with its power to dissolve ions, plays a key part in the battery. Zinc, for example, is more easily ionised than copper and dissolves in the electrolyte as positive ions, leaving some of its electrons behind. These surplus electrons can be drained off, through an external circuit round to the other electrode, where they can join ions such as hydrogen, coming from the electrolyte, and neutralise them, so completing the circuit. This process can keep going so long as some zinc remains to dissolve.

These electrolytic effects, which depend on the different chemical reactivities of various substances, are of course used in many practical ways: in batteries, in electroplating and, usually with molten salt electrolytes, in the manufacture of aluminium, sodium, chlorine, hydrogen, and other substances. The basic laws of electrolysis were worked out by Faraday who compared the amounts of substance reacted with the amounts of electricity transferred to show that the ions carry units of charge; these are of course the same units as belong to the electron, since the underlying process is the separation or combination of ions with electrons. The unit of electric current is the *ampere*, a flow of one *coulomb* of electric charge per second, and one coulomb is equivalent to about 6 million million million electrons. The 'pumping power' of a battery, i.e. the electric *potential* which drives the electrons round a circuit from one terminal to the other, is measured by the *volt*. A single cell of a copper-zinc battery develops a potential of just over 1 volt.

The Electrical Nature of Magnetism

The other big discovery early in the 19th century was that magnetism is related to electricity. Magnetism had of course been known for centuries, from the fact that 'lodestones', like pieces of iron after stroking with other magnets, exerted forces on one another, could pick up iron, and pointed north when freely hung. In the 16th century Gilbert realised that the earth itself is a great bar magnet, aligned more or less along its north-south axis. But no connection with electricity was seen until Oersted showed in 1819 that a current could deflect a magnetic compass sideways across its wire. Faraday in 1831 then found the complementary effect, *magnetic induction*, in which for example a wire coil generates an electric current while a magnet is being plunged through it. Faraday also vividly demonstrated *magnetic* fields of force through the patterns made by iron filings sprinkled near magnets.

The interplay between electricity and magnetism appears only when there is *motion*; a current changing; a magnet moving. And in fact it was the consideration of electromagnetic effects that led Einstein to his special relativity, which is of course a theory of motion. By reversing this story, we can use relativity to show that magnetism is an aspect of electricity.

Imagine a long straight wire carrying a steady current. We are at rest alongside it and can think of it as two long parallel columns of charge; a fixed column of positive ions – the wire itself – and a mobile column of negative electrons sliding along it. We find the wire to be uncharged and so conclude that the abundance of the electrons along it is the same as that of the ions.

Now suppose that outside the wire there is a negative

charge, moving along parallel to it. For simplicity let this charge keep pace with the electrons moving along inside the wire, although this assumption is not strictly necessary. What do we find? That this charge is pulled towards the wire. To see why, let us move along the wire, together with the charge. To us now, this charge is static. The force pulling it to the wire must, then, be an electric one since this is the force that static charges feel. We must conclude that, from our moving viewpoint, the wire appears as *positively charged*, since it is attracting the negative charge.

The basis for this effect is the relativistic contraction of length. We saw in chapter 2 that a moving length appears to be contracted in its direction of motion. From our moving viewpoint, the positive column is now moving and hence *contracted*. Conversely, the negative column is now at rest and hence *extended*, compared with what it was before. As a result, there appear to be more positive charges and fewer negative ones in unit length of wire than before. Since the magnitude of a charge is unchanged by motion, it follows that the wire now has a net positive charge, according to our new viewpoint, and so attracts the external charge.

Let us now return to our old viewpoint, at rest relative to the wire. The wire is now uncharged but the attraction of the moving external charge, and hence the force, is still there. In this viewpoint we can no longer ascribe it to electro-statics and so we have to regard it as a new electrical force, due to the *current* of charge in the wire; we call it a *magnetic force*.

The argument could be given more generally, for an external charge moving in some arbitrary direction relative to the wire. When we take its direction of motion into account, we find that various directional features appear in the magnetic force. In fact, we have to picture circular magnetic field lines, round the wire as their axis, and their effect on a moving external charge brings in all the space axes, as well as time. In the above simple example

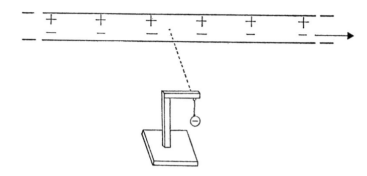

A current-carrying wire exerts no electrical force on a stationary test charge, because the spacing of the negative charges moving along the wire is the same as that of the positive charges at rest in the wire.

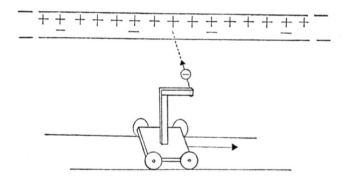

But when the test charge moves along the same wire, keeping pace with the moving negative charges, it feels an electrical force from the wire, which now appears to be positively charged. This is because the *Lorentz Contraction* of special relativity reduces the perceived spacing of the positive charges and increases that of the negative ones, so that there are now more positive than negative charges in unit length of the wire. This force is the *Magnetic* force.

the charge moving along the wire cuts the magnetic field lines at right angles and feels a force towards the wire, i.e. at right angles to both its direction of motion and to the field line it is cutting. This force at right angles to both the motion and the field is characteristic of electromagnetism and there are systematic rules for working it out in various situations.

We have found magnetism from electricity, but to get it in a more familiar form let us wind the wire into coils. Take a cylindrical stick and, at its bottom end, begin winding the coil round it. When about half the wire is so wound, run the remaining wire a little way up the stick before continuing to wind the rest of it into a second coil, the same way round as before. The second coil is thus a direct continuation of the first, a little farther up. Because of the way they are wound, the current passes round both in the same direction. We then have, in effect, two circular rotating rings of electrons, one above the other, all going the same way round. The forces from the stationary positive ions cancel the 'electrostatic' part of the forces from the moving electrons, leaving only the 'magnetic' part, due to the movement of the electrons, outstanding. By our argument above, the two rings attract each other through their magnetic force, acting in the direction of the magnetic field lines. In fact, the upper face of the bottom coil attracts the lower face of the top coil. At this point, we might as well begin calling the upper and lower faces of a coil 'north' and 'south', respectively. If we turn one of the coils upside down, so that its electrons now run the other way round, we get north facing north between the two coils, or south facing south, giving a repulsion. This is just like bar magnets! In fact, if we stretch each coil out into a long spiral, it becomes a *solenoid* electromagnet. Moreover, if we strain such a solenoid into two parts, by pulling its middle few turns out straight, it becomes two electromagnets, each with a north and south face, just as happens when we break an iron bar magnet into two, across its middle. In an iron magnet, in fact, the magnetism is due to a particular motion of some of the electrons inside the metal.

We have seen then that magnetism is a relativistic effect of moving charge. The electrons in a metal move quickly, but mainly bounce to and fro, so that the net velocity with which they drift down a wire, to give an electric current, is quite small, typically only about one ten-thousandth of a metre per second. Relativistic effects always develop in proportion to the square of the speed divided by the square of the speed of light. We might thus be forgiven for thinking that we could neglect a relativistic effect as small as we have in this case. But this would be wrong. Magnetism is a small modification of the enormously strong electrical force of nature, and so is quite strong compared, say, with gravitation. Furthermore, the direct electrical force of the electrons in the wire is almost totally neutralised by that of the positive ions, so that the magnetic force is left to display itself as the only effect outstanding from the current in the wire.

Although small, compared with the intrinsic electrical forces, the magnetic force can be powerful. It is the basis of all heavy electrical machinery. It drives great electric motors, produces enormous amounts of electricity from turbogenerators, and is able to levitate, by 'magnetic suspension', whole trains and float them along, above an electrical track. Essentially, we have three interlinked things in all these applications: electricity, magnetism, and motion. Given any two of these, and a suitable source of energy such as a waterfall or a steam engine, we can always produce the third, which is the basis of the electrical power industry.

The Electrical Nature of Light

In the theory of relativity a new effect – gravitation – is brought in by changing from uniform to accelerated motion.

It is the same in electromagnetism; the new effect that acceleration brings this time is *radiation*, including light. The speed of light turns up inevitably, of course, in the relativistic theory of electromagnetism. Actually, a speed of just this value appeared much earlier in the history of the subject, from the relative strengths of electrostatic and electromagnetic forces, but its significance was missed until Maxwell, in 1864, deduced that oscillating electromagnetic fields could spread through space at this speed, and that light itself is exactly such a field. This discovery of the electrical nature of light, a great advance in our understanding of nature, was endorsed soon afterwards by the brilliant experiments of Hertz, who made the first radio waves and showed that they had just the same properties as light, at a longer wavelength.

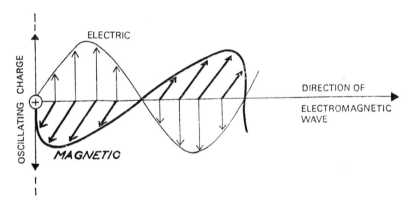

An electric charge oscillates up and down, radiating electromagnetic waves. The lines of electric force act up and down. Those of magnetic force act in and out, at right angles to the electric field. Both sets of field lines are at right angles to the direction of advance of the electromagnetic wave.

An electromagnetic wave is made by shaking an electric charge to and fro. This is what happens in a transmitter aerial. The moving electrical field of this charge makes a magnetic field nearby. This magnetic field, because it also is moving, makes an electric field; and so on. In this way, two pulsating and interlinked fields induce each other to spread farther and farther forward, so moving out into space of their own accord, as free fields independent of their source. The electromagnetic wave involves all three axes of space, as well as time. There is first the direction in which it is advancing forward. At right angles to this are the other two axes, a 'vertical' one along which one of the fields – say the electric – exerts its force; and the 'horizontal' one along which the other – magnetic – field similarly acts. The vertical electrical force oscillates up and down and the sideways magnetic force equally oscillates from side to side. These are both *transverse* oscillations, like those along a slightly slack rope shaken to and fro across itself from one end, and the two sets of waves, one vertical, the other horizontal, spread forward together as an inseparable pair, forming the complete electromagnetic wave.

Oscillation is a kind of acceleration and so we have to look at the fields of accelerating charges. It will be useful to notice first something curious about the field of a *uniformly* moving charge. Suppose that such a charge is moving at constant speed across our view, some way off. Accepting that its field travels with the speed of light, we expect that this field comes to us, not from the 'present' position of the charge at the time when the field reaches us, but from the 'time-retarded' position where the charge was at the earlier time when the field started out. This in fact is exactly what happens. However, nature tries to conceal it from us. To see why, we turn the problem round by supposing that the distant charge is at rest and that we are moving instead, uniformly through its now *static* field. This field appears to us, as with all things, to be relativistically contracted in the direction of our motion, but there can no longer be any question of a retarded position. The field is now merely that of the charge in its present position, because the charge, being at rest, is in this position all the time! The directions of the forces felt from it, on test charges we prudently happen to have brought along with us, would leave us in no doubt that the static field of the fixed charge is centred on this position. This present position is nevertheless *not* where we would *see* the charge, i.e. it is not the direction from where we would find electromagnetic radiation coming from it, because the *aberration* effect discussed in chapter 2 would cause us to sight it farther back; exactly at the retarded position in fact!

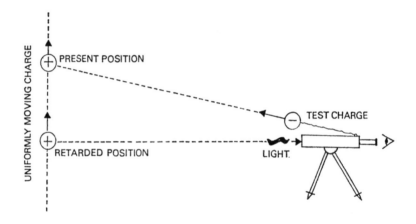

An electrical charge, moving uniformly across the line of sight, is seen 'to be' at its retarded position, where it was when the light started out from it. But its electrical force is felt to come from its present position, where it is when the light reaches the observer.

Going back to our original viewpoint again, and so ascribing the motion to the charge, not ourselves, we would still find the static field to be centred on its present position, since all we have done is to change the way we choose to describe the same situation. The field is nevertheless coming from the retarded position and, if we were to work through the calculations, we would discover that a particular factor comes in which adds on to the retarded field in such a way

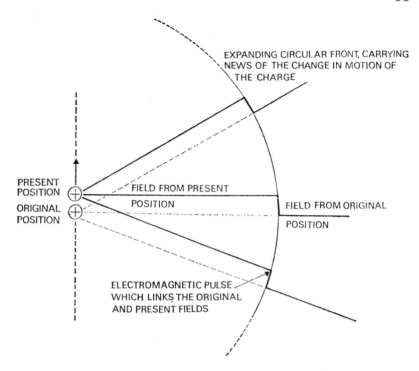

EXPANDING CIRCULAR FRONT, CARRYING NEWS OF THE CHANGE IN MOTION OF THE CHARGE

PRESENT POSITION

ORIGINAL POSITION

FIELD FROM PRESENT POSITION

FIELD FROM ORIGINAL POSITION

ELECTROMAGNETIC PULSE WHICH LINKS THE ORIGINAL AND PRESENT FIELDS

After resting for a long time in its original position, an electrical charge is given a pulse of acceleration which sets it into uniform motion (upwards) thereafter. The news of this pulse of acceleration spreads out circularly, at the speed of light, from the charge. At any point outside this circle the electrical field is felt to come from the original position; and, at any point inside, it is felt to come from the present position. When the expanding circle sweeps through any given point, the field there suddenly changes as it readjusts from the original to the present position of the charge. The electro-magnetic pulse which accomplishes this change is a pulse of *radiation*.

as to make this seem as if it is coming from the present position.

We can now turn to *acceleration*. Suppose that we are at rest and that the same distant charge has been sitting at rest, by our reckoning, for a long time. And that then, for a very short time, say during the period of 1 second, it accelerates to a certain speed across our line of sight, which it thereafter holds constant. The electromagnetic message of this brief acceleration comes to us at the speed of light. While it is on its way, the charge continues moving with its newly acquired constant velocity, so that by the time the message reaches us, it can have shifted to a present position a long way from its original one.

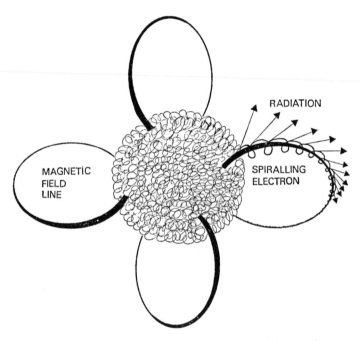

Possible process of radiation from a quasar. Lines of magnetic force loop out from the hot envelope of gas round the quasar. High-speed electrons are shot out and spiral round the magnetic lines, emitting 'synchrotron' radiation.

What do we experience of all this? At first we simply feel the static field of the charge at rest in its *original* position. Then the message arrives. There is 1 second of hiatus, after which we experience the steady field of the uniformly moving charge. But we feel this field as if it were coming from the *present* position of the charge, not the original one, even though we 'see' the charge only just beginning to move away from its original position. During the 1 second of hiatus, then, there is a drastic change as the field rapidly swings from its original position to its present one. A drastic and rapid change of electric field implies a strong magnetic field, and vice versa, so that the hiatus consists of a 1 second surge of electromagnetic field, which is much stronger than the steady fields which precede and follow it. This surge is *radiation*, the additional and freely propagating field produced by the short acceleration of the charge. It comes to us of course from the original position of the charge, just as light comes from the retarded positions of distant, moving objects.

In these days of radio, telecommunications and radar, the practical applications of electromagnetic radiation are obvious, and it is of course also through such radiation that we see things and enjoy the sun's rays. There are various natural processes by which charges radiate. To take just one, an electron moving through a magnetic field tends to circle round the magnetic field lines – trying to pick up the motion of the charged source of those lines, as it were. A strong magnetic field pulls the circles very tight and, if the electron is going at relativistic speeds, this rapid circling is a form of violent acceleration – as if we were driving in a high-speed car round a small circus ring – and the electron in consequence generates large amounts of radiant energy. This process, called *synchrotron radiation*, seems to be the way in which spinning neutron stars and violent centres of galaxies pour out their enormous amounts of radiation. The conditions there are right for this, with enormously strong magnetic fields and charged particles speeding almost like light itself.

6

The Grain of Things

Intimations of Atomicity

Two thousand years ago, Lucretius in his great poem *Of the Nature of Things* imagined matter as a multitude of particles, too small to be seen, in rapid motion. This idea, already then a few hundred years old, had to struggle right up into this century before being finally accepted. Opposing it were those who believed that matter was continuous – that we could, at least in principle, go on dividing up, say, a drop of water into smaller drops, repeated times without end, and these would always be recognisable as water, able to be divided up still more. There were also the sceptics who simply would not believe what they could not see. A long struggle, but it has given us our greatest single discovery about the physical world: its *atomicity*.

Today's powerful scientific instruments have of course made atomicity a plain fact. But is there any way of convincing ourselves about it, from more familiar experiences? The great atomists of the 19th century, in their theories of chemistry and of gases, reached their conclusions by long chains of intricate reasoning – as far from the everyday world, in their way, as today's particle accelerators. The basic difficulty of course is that the wavelength of ordinary light is too coarse to enable us to focus on a single atom or molecule in a microscope. The best we can do with ordinary light is to scatter it sideways off fine particles, as for example when a sunbeam is revealed by a cloud of fine tobacco smoke drifting across it. Very small particles, down to about a millionth of a centimetre across, can be tracked in a microscope by this means. These are well above atomic size but will show something discovered by the botanist Brown in 1827. He saw minute grains of pollen in water zigzagging about ceaselessly in a state of random motion. This effect, which is shown by all sufficiently fine particles of matter in any clear fluid or in air, remained a mystery until about 80 years later when it was seen to be direct evidence for molecular motion. A speck of cigarette smoke floating in the air is struck repeatedly in every direction by the air molecules. In this random bombardment there are occasions when the rain of tiny blows on one side of the speck chances to be slightly fiercer than on the other, and the speck is then driven sideways. As the direction of the onslaught fluctuates so the speck is driven wildly to and fro. Remarkably, one can analyse this haphazard motion mathematically, to deduce from it the number of molecules in a cubic centimetre of air, which is 3 followed by 19 noughts.

From this we can also deduce the size of a molecule, for if we liquefy air by extreme cooling, it contracts to about half a thousandth of its gaseous volume. Liquids, including liquid air, are rather incompressible and so we suppose that their volume is that of their molecules, crowded closely together. Thus we find that a molecule is a few *angstroms* across (a hundred million angstroms equal one centimetre). It is hard to grasp the immenseness of the numbers of molecules there are in ordinary pieces of matter. If an apple were magnified to the size of the earth, its water molecules would then be the size of apples. If the molecules in a raindrop were laid out side by side, in a single straight line, this line would easily reach from here to the sun.

A fairly familiar indication of molecular sizes is given by the spreading of oil on water. A drop of, say, olive oil placed on clean water quickly spreads into a large round patch, as can be seen by its brushing aside particles of talc already dusted on the water as markers. The effect is quite systematic; the patch grows to a fixed area of about 1 square metre per cubic millimetre of oil drop. Lord Rayleigh argued that the oil stopped spreading when its film became one molecule thick and he thus estimated the molecular size by dividing the droplet volume by the film area.

We have spoken above of both atoms and molecules. The distinction between these takes us on to *chemistry*. Centuries of experiments in which substances were mixed, dissolved, boiled, burnt, distilled and crystallised, leading from the mystical gropings of the alchemists to the systematic investigations of Priestley and Lavoisier, had shown by the end of the 18th century that all material things were combinations of a small number of primary substances, the chemical *elements* such as hydrogen, oxygen, iron and sulphur. If a piece of, say, iron is divided up into the smallest particles which are still recognisable as iron – for example, from their spectroscopic signature, discussed in chapter 2 – these are single atoms of the element. If a piece of a chemical *compound* is similarly divided, without chemical change, we arrive at the smallest example of that compound, a molecule in which the atoms of the component elements are clustered. The water molecule, for example, is two hydrogen atoms joined to one oxygen atom.

The 90 or so different naturally existing chemical elements are nature's alphabet, from which a great dictionary of different words – the molecules – is written and which exist in enormous numbers to produce the infinite variety of the world – the libraries, as it were. Lucretius sensed something of this when he compared atoms to letters and said 'scattered abroad in my verses you see many letters common to many words, and yet you must needs grant that verses and words are unlike in sense and in the ring of their sound'. For the modern view we turn to John Dalton who saw, at the beginning of the 19th century, that the regularities by which elements combined together to form compounds could be most easily understood if the elements consisted of atoms; and that the compounds were formed by the union of a few atoms – the same always, for the same compound – of the constituent elements. By this step, he opened the way to both modern chemistry and modern atomic theory. It was crucial to his argument that all the atoms of a given element were *identical*, an idea which, after absorbing a later modification (isotopic variants of an atom), has become basic to our picture of the world. Lucretius anticipated it with his analogy; for any letter 'a' in a written work is indistinguishable in its function from any other 'a'; it is always an 'a', a whole 'a' and nothing but an 'a'. This is how nature is at the atomic level; particles are either strictly identical or quite different.

The Social Life of Atoms

The cohesion of a raindrop, the hardness of diamond, the fortitude of a storm-lashed headland, the strength of the steel cable which prevents our lift from entertaining us with Einstein's free-fall, the compression of commuters on a crowded train – all these testify to the forces between atoms, the attractions that bind atoms to one another and the repulsions by which each atom resists too close an approach by neighbours. These powerful forces are all 'short-range'. There is no question of an inverse-square law here. If you bring two lumps of rock together you feel no force between them until they touch. Special methods (welding) are needed to make metals adhere, but, once they do, the united lumps then resist separation with all their traditional strengths.

The attractive forces between different atoms vary enormously. For some, such as helium, neon and argon, they are almost non-existent and these atoms mainly exist as solitary individuals, in a chemically uncombined state. Other atoms tend to join together in small numbers to form molecules

which then have little affinity for one another. The chemical
bond in these is said to have been *saturated*. Many familiar
substances are of this kind: e.g. the atom-pair molecules of
nitrogen, oxygen and hydrogen; the three oxygen atoms of
ozone; the single oxygen and two hydrogen atoms of water;
the single carbon and two oxygen atoms of carbon dioxide;
and the single nitrogen and three hydrogen atoms of ammonia.

Residual forces between chemically inactive atoms and
molecules can cause these to settle at low temperatures into
large groups, as in water and ice, or in the various oils and
waxes, and the substances of the organic world. Other substances go farther in this direction and the distinction between
the main chemical forces and the residual ones eventually
disappears. In other words, in these substances the chemical
bond is *unsaturatable*, and there is then no limit to the number
of atoms or molecules which can be joined together strongly.
This is the world of the inorganic minerals, the silicates in
rocks, the salt crystals, diamonds, and metals.

It is helpful to think about the relations between atoms in
terms of *energy* rather than forces. The basic idea is quite
simple. In the same way as energy is needed to lift a weight
away from the earth, against the force of gravity, so it is
needed to lift molecules or atoms away from one another,
against their attractive forces; and the amount required is a
measure of the strength and range of these forces. For example,
to go on boiling water in a kettle, forcing its molecules apart
into steam, you have to go on supplying heat to it, putting in
about 500 calories of 'latent heat' for each cubic centimetre
vaporised.

There is an interesting connection with raindrops here.
When we vaporise a body of water into steam we take each
molecule completely away from its neighbours. When, instead, we smear out a drop of water on a dry surface we take
it part way towards the vaporised state since we increase the
number of its molecules at its surface, where they have no

neighbours on one side; a little of the latent heat is needed for this, in the form of 'surface energy'. The energy involved in making a small water drop 'sit up' in defiance of gravity is clearly miniscule compared with the latent heat to vaporise the drop, which implies that only a small proportion of the molecules are at the surface and hence that the molecules are very small. The surface energy in fact is a few millionths of a calorie per square centimetre. Thus a one centimetre cube of water, i.e. 500 calories worth of latent heat, should be convertible to about one hundred million square centimetres of surface, on this energy argument, which once more brings us to the characteristic scale of the angstrom for molecular sizes.

The *Brownian motion* vividly shows the kinetic nature of heat. We picture a multitude of atoms or molecules all moving ceaselessly to and fro, jostling and bouncing off one another in all directions, and we simply lump the mechanical energies of these chaotic movements all together as *heat*. The amount of this heat depends both on how many particles are involved in this chaotic motion – i.e. on the *capacity* of the system – and on the vigour of their individual motions, which we experience as the *temperature* of the system. If the temperature is low enough, the particles cluster together closely, making a liquid or solid. We picture a particle clinging to a cluster but-being shaken to and fro by the thermal agitation. The higher the temperature, the farther away it can oscillate, like a pendulum bob swinging more wildly as its energy of motion is increased, until eventually it may fly right off and escape, to become a particle of vapour or gas. The escape of atoms from molecules, generally at much higher temperatures, is another example of this same disruptive effect of heat.

The extent to which it happens depends of course on the temperature in relation to the binding energies of the particles. Here on earth we are used to a temperature at which nitrogen, oxygen and carbon dioxide are all molecular gases; i.e. it is warm enough to keep the molecules apart but not to break them up into separate atoms. It is also a temperature at which water is nicely poised between the vaporised, liquid and frozen states; at which the inorganic minerals are mostly solid; and at which organic molecules are fairly mobile and chemically active. We take all this for granted, but of the other planets only Mars has conditions even remotely like our own.

A crucial point about heat energy is that, at any instant, it is shared *unequally* among the atomic and molecular motions. As an atom jostles with its neighbours, it is sometimes stopped in its tracks and sometimes knocked forwards more strongly than before. It is like a gambler, winning and losing on successive throws of the dice, rich one moment and poor the next, but never excluded from the game even when temporarily 'broke'. Most of the time its personal energy fortune hovers at about the average of its companions. But occasionally it may have a lucky run of wins and temporarily acquire a fortune. Outstanding runs are rare, however, so that in the multitude at any instant there are few 'energy millionaires' and extremely few multi-millionaires. The laws of gambling operate just as inexorably here. Very roughly, about one particle in a thousand has seven times the average energy, one in a million has fourteen times, and so on. This is for a single motion of a single particle. For a particle moving or vibrating in all three dimensions of space – and still more for a molecule whose atoms also jostle one another – a high energy won in one particular form of motion is usually matched by more nondescript luck in the other forms, so that its overall fluctuations are less dramatic.

This unequal sharing is important because it enables a multitude of particles to explore every conceivable configuration and combination within reach of their total energy. This opens the way to nature's infinite variety. The ceaseless random movement of the atoms and molecules, bringing them together in all possible arrangements, a few with energies which in a large multitude may be far above average, enables all molecular configurations and states of matter, even bizarre ones, to be tried out. Most of these are unstable of course and fall apart almost as soon as they are made. But, as one falls apart, somewhere else in the multitude another may be thrown together. And if one of these randomly formed extravaganzas shows some stability, even though its particles may have gone through unstable forms on the way, it will tend to survive and a few of its kind may then exist as characteristic features of the system.

In some cases, survival is greatly aided by physical separation. We see this in the formation of a vapour above a liquid or solid. All may be at the same temperature, but the particles of the vapour nevertheless have more energy than their companions in the condensed substance; for they have the potential energy by which they escaped from its attractive forces, which we know as latent heat. Having escaped, some will chance to fly back again and get recaptured. But others may fly right away and survive for long times, like the water molecules of moist air blown in from distant oceans where they were evaporated. The sparseness of particles in a vapour, compared with their abundance in the condensed state, shows directly the rarity of large energy fluctuations; such particles are sparse because they are precisely those rare energy millionaires who happen to have used their winnings to escape from the condensed state.

The uneven sharing of energy is also seen in the earth's atmosphere. Air fills a room evenly everywhere and its pressure is the overall result of its molecules crashing into the walls and bouncing back off them, like innumerable little bullets. But the atmosphere is open to space! However, in climbing high, the molecules have to do work against gravity and so we find a thin atmosphere containing only a few (potential energy) millionaires, at high altitudes. An interesting point here is that the gravitational energy at a given height is smaller for light molecules than heavy ones, which is why there is practically no free hydrogen or helium in the atmosphere. Being so light, their particles are much more easily able to escape from the earth than those of the heavier gases, oxygen, nitrogen, carbon dioxide, and water vapour.

In a condensed substance the attractive forces between the particles are strong enough to keep the thermal motion partly under control. In a pure element or compound the atoms or molecules, being all the same, generally behave all in the same way. In particular, each positions itself in the same place in relation to its neighbours, like a soldier on parade. This is what happens in *crystallisation*, in which the particles line up into regular patterns, spread through the three dimensions of space like the patterns in two dimensions of wallpapers or soldiers on parade. In such a *crystal lattice* the particles are set out regularly in lines; these lines are similarly arranged regularly in planes, and these planes again are stacked regularly on top of one another to make the crystal. Because there is no geometric 'end' to such a crystal structure, the crystal can grow to unlimited size simply by the addition of more particles to it, all in the same arrangement.

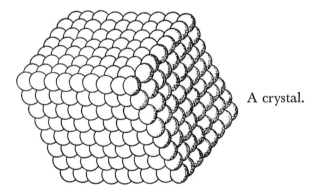

A crystal.

Crystals are nature's ornaments. The brilliance of diamond, ruby and emerald, the pellucidity of rock crystal, the symmetry of crystal facets, the sharp straight edges and exact angles, have long excited great interest as well as admiration, which made crystallography one of the oldest of the sciences. Many familiar substances also are crystalline, such as common salt, sugar, and metals. The metals in fact have some of the simplest crystal structures of all, such as can be modelled by stacking tennis balls together in closely packed orderly patterns. We do not ordinarily notice the crystallinity of metals, however, because everyday pieces consist of masses of microcrystals whose external shape bears no relation to their internal symmetry. Unlike the brittle mineral crystals, which can usually be split by cleavage along symmetry planes through the material, metal crystals are generally *ductile*, which means that when a strong force is brought to bear on them, their atoms yield to it by sliding along the symmetry planes instead of cleaving apart. This is what happens when we crumple a sheet of aluminium foil, bend a nail, or dent a car.

Because of their regularity, the structures of crystals can be studied in the most marvellous detail by the *diffraction of X-rays*. We remember the basic effect from chapter 2. Rays from a distant source are scattered through the interstices of a fine lattice structure – such as is provided by a silk screen, in the case of light – only into certain specific directions, those along which the waves coming from different scattering centres fit together neatly, crest to crest. The wavelengths of X-rays are just right for diffraction from crystal lattices, where the centres are spaced at the atomic scale of distances, and the patterns produced by X-ray diffraction experiments have now told us the exact arrangements, shapes and sizes of the atoms in a vast number of crystals, as well as in many molecules that can be made to crystallise. It is even possible to map out the distribution of electrons in various parts of a crystal structure – showing the atoms as round balls of negative electricity, slightly fuzzy at their edges where one seems to merge into the next – as well as to study the oscillations of the atoms and to examine the faults which occasionally occur in the regular packing of the atoms.

Liquids are nature's surprise. We can see why gases exist, at high temperatures where the thermal forces are too strong for the atomic or molecular bonds; and also why crystals exist, at low temperatures where the particles are commanded by the bonding forces into an orderly packing. But why is there a second kind of condensed matter, the liquid, almost as dense as the crystal and almost as disorderly as the gas? The answer seems to lie in a rather subtle effect. If we compress a gas, while keeping its temperature constant, its pressure rises at first because its particles hit the walls more frequently, like tennis balls rebounding between opponents who are advancing from the baseline to volley at the net. But as we compress it still more densely the pressure does not rise quite so steeply because at this stage the particles, being now fairly close together, spend a lot of their time in range of one another's attractive forces. As the density rises still further, these attractive forces may eventually take over the task of compression completely, pulling the particles together from the inside, so sparing us the burden of pushing from the outside. The possibility of this depends on the temperature. Above a critical temperature, the attractive forces always need some external backing to resist the thermal forces. The substance then remains a gas, even at high densities. Below this temperature they can manage on their own to hold the particles together in a compact crowd. The key point is that this self-contained state must have such a structure as will allow it to merge smoothly into that of the externally contained state, because the distinction between them gradually fades away as the critical temperature is approached. A liquid, with its disorganised gas-like structure, can do this, but a crystal with its regular lattice structure, could not possibly do so. We see then that a liquid state is necessary because the continuity at the critical temperature requires a smooth transition from the gas to a condensed state. A liquid thus does not differ from a gas fundamentally in its structure, but in its mechanical behaviour, i.e. in the fact that it can hold its *volume* stable without external help.

There is a corresponding distinction between liquids and solids. If a liquid is cooled down sufficiently far, without crystallising, its particles may not have enough heat energy to be able to slide over each other and allow it to flow. It can then hold its *shape* stable without external help and we say that it is *solid*. Glass at room temperature is an example. Unfortunately, the word 'solid' is often used interchangeably with 'crystalline'. The real distinctions are between disordered (liquid and gaseous) and crystalline substances, in terms of *structure*; between gaseous and condensed (liquid and crystalline) substances in terms of stability of *volume*; and between fluids (gases and mobile liquids) and solids (crystals and stiff liquids) in terms of stability of *shape*.

The Heart of Matter

X-ray diffraction shows atoms as small spherical clouds of electrons. But where is the positive charge, which neutralises the electrons; or the heavy mass, which the light electrons cannot provide? Those questions were answered by Rutherford's beautiful experiments. Following the discoveries by Becquerel and the Curies of the radioactively produced radiations, given off by elements such as uranium and radium, he became particularly interested in using *alpha particles*, one of the three such radiations, as probes into the structure of matter. Alpha particles are four times as heavy as hydrogen atoms, and in fact are helium atoms in the form of positive ions, lacking the two electrons that make them neutral. They are shot out of radioactively disintegrating atoms at great speed, over one-twentieth of that of light, and go through everything in their way. It requires about three inches of air or a thick sheet of paper to stop one. For Rutherford they were ideal 'bullets' to shoot into matter, especially as they could be spotted from the tiny flashes of light produced where they struck a 'scintillation screen' of zinc sulphide; and later could be tracked from the 'vapour trails' they produced when passing through chilled damp air in a 'cloud chamber'.

Rutherford found that these heavy particles, fired at thin metal foils, generally ploughed straight through millions of atoms, brushing aside the numerous light electrons in their way, although gradually slowed down by the sheer weight of numbers of these. Evidently, apart from the feeble resistance put up by its electrons, an atom is extremely transparent to a high-speed alpha particle. But Rutherford also found that about one particle in 10,000 suffered a major collision during its passage, being sharply turned into a quite different direction. To him it was like seeing an artillery shell bounce back from a sheet of tissue paper! By studying the numbers of such deflections at various angles he located, at the centre of the atom, the heavy small target – the *nucleus* – off which an alpha particle rebounds on the rare occasions when it happens to hit this minute bull's-eye. He also found that the nuclei were positively charged and that the alpha particles were deflected by electrical repulsion, Coulomb's law being accurately obeyed even at the extremely small distances, within one ten-thousandth of an atomic diameter, at which the collisions occurred.

And so the nuclear atom was discovered: an extremely small positively charged nucleus containing most of the atomic mass, surrounded by electrons swarming around it, in sufficient numbers to neutralise its charge. But what about the 90 or so different chemical elements? These all have different nuclei, but are there no common features between them? Many years earlier, the chemists had noticed that atoms combined in proportion to their *atomic weights*, and that these were often nearly equal to the weight of several hydrogen atoms, which suggested that the heavier ones might be multiples of hydrogen. Then, also in the 19th century, Mendeleev made his great discovery of the *Periodic Table*: that if you write down all the elements in order of increasing atomic weight, their chemical properties repeat at intervals along the list; for example, *sodium* comes eight elements after the similar metal *lithium,* and *chlorine* comes eight after *fluorine.*

The serial number in this list – the *atomic number* – became important when it was later discovered to be also the number of electrons in the neutral atom; or, equivalently, the number of unit positive charges in the nucleus. The key to the individual chemical properties of the elements lay here. But there was also a puzzle. Moving along the list, the atomic weight·increases much faster than the atomic number. For the lightest atom, hydrogen, the atomic weight and number are both unity. But the second element helium, with atomic number 2, already weighs 4 times as much as hydrogen, as we have seen. And so it goes on, up to the 92nd naturally occurring element, uranium, which weighs about 238 times as much.

The cluster of protons and neutrons in a large atomic nucleus.

If atomic nuclei contain hydrogen nuclei, which we now call *protons* – and Rutherford proved this in 1919 by knocking them out of nuclei with his alpha particles – what in the nucleus makes up the balance between mass and charge? This question was answered by Chadwick's discovery in 1932 of the *neutron,* the second particle in the nucleus, almost identical with the proton but with no electrical charge.

For a few years, our picture of the structure of matter had then reached its state of greatest simplicity. The nucleus was a small, tightly packed, cluster of protons and neutrons. The total number of these gave the weight of the atom; and the number of protons gave the nuclear charge, neutralised by the same number of electrons flying around in the space outside the nucleus, and from which the chemical properties were derived. All nuclei with the same number of protons belong to the same chemical element, but they can have different numbers of neutrons, in which case they are called *isotopes* of that element. The whole of nature, the immense variety of everything, was so reduced to the various inter-plays of just three kinds of 'elementary particle' and electro-magnetic and gravitational interactions! Since then, the picture has been getting complicated again and today we know of a whole array of other, recently discovered and ill-understood, particles.

The atomic nucleus remains however a cluster of protons and neutrons held together by some force, which must be extremely strong to hold the protons so closely against their electrostatic repulsion. It is so strong in fact that the energy it releases, mainly as gamma rays, when protons and neutrons unite to form a nucleus, is enough to change their mass noticeably by Einstein's mass-energy relation. For example, the two protons and two neutrons of helium, which happens to be a particularly stable nucleus, weigh nearly 1 per cent less than the 4 separate particles. The release of this mass, as energy, by the uniting of hydrogen nuclei (with nuclear transformations involving other particles, to convert some protons to neutrons) is the basis of the thermonuclear power which runs the stars.

The nuclear force has an extremely short range. It is all-powerful within the nucleus, at distances within about one hundred-thousandth of the atomic diameter, but almost negligible at slightly greater ranges. We have already met something like this in the short-range forces between atoms and molecules – although of a very different nature – and it turns out in fact that nuclei behave in some ways like water drops. Very small nuclear droplets are only moderately stable because practically all of their few particles are then in their surfaces and so are on the way towards 'evaporation'. Large ones also are not the most stable, because the electrical repulsions between their numerous protons try hard to spring them apart, which is why spontaneous radioactivity is found among the heaviest atoms. The alpha particles are splinters from such nuclei, pushed out by the protons of the remainder. The most stable nuclei are of intermediate size, in elements such as iron.

Many nuclei can be excited into radioactivity by bombardment with nuclear particles. In the simplest cases they are just violently shaken by the collision and during their ensuing pulsations may throw off pulses of energy, i.e. gamma radiation. In other cases, a bombarding particle may enter and become part of the nucleus, inducing transformations in it directly. Neutrons are powerful inducers of nuclear reactions. When a neutron gets into the uranium-235 nucleus (i.e. with 92 protons and 143 neutrons) it causes this rather large and flexible 'drop' to wobble and eventually break into two nearly equal parts, together with one or two spare neutrons. This is the *fission* process, the basis of nuclear electric power.

All these effects are due to the interplay of the powerful nuclear and electrical forces. The gravitational force, negligible in such atomic nuclei, comes into its own when old stars collapse to extreme densities. The neutron star is a gigantic atomic nucleus held together by gravitation. In such a vast cluster of nuclear particles as this, only a very few can be protons, otherwise the electrical repulsion would be overwhelming. As the atoms crush down, during the gravitational collapse to nuclear density, a wholesale conversion of protons and electrons to neutrons must take place.

Origin of the Elements

By far the most abundant element in the universe is hydrogen. Protons are particularly stable forms of nuclear matter and measurements of the reactivities of various nuclear particles lead to the conclusion that, as the fledgling universe emerged from the big bang, while its temperature still exceeded 1,000,000,000° c. most of its positive charge would have taken the form of protons.

In this sense, then, the early atomic chemists were right; all the other nuclei have come from the fusing together of protons, together with the various concomitant nuclear transformations to make neutrons from protons and other particles. The barrier to nuclear fusion is the electrical repulsion which holds positive particles apart at distances beyond reach of the attractive nuclear force. To break through this barrier the particles have to be thrown together violently. In the laboratory we can do this with particle accelerators, but in nature the main source of such violent motion is heat energy. The temperatures needed are very high, hundreds of millions of degrees for a rapid reaction.

The two possibilities for such temperatures are the big bang itself, and the insides of stars. The first step in the synthesis of the higher elements is the formation of helium from four hydrogen nuclei, a process which itself involves a series of simpler nuclear reactions. Most of the energy of the stars comes from making helium, but calculations show that in the galaxy hardly more than one atom in 100 need be helium to account for all the energy poured out from it since its creation, whereas in fact about one-tenth of the atoms are helium. This leads to the conclusion that most of the helium in the universe was made in the big bang (about 100 seconds after it started, in fact!), as originally suggested by Gamow, whose calculations showed that the conditions then were quite suitable for this.

For fusion, the particles must not only move about

energetically; they must meet! This presented no difficulty for making helium in the big bang, but the early universe almost certainly did not stay in its dense, hot, state for long enough to allow much helium 'burning' to take place. All the heavier elements were probably made in stars, as was shown convincingly by the calculations of Burbidge, Burbidge, Fowler and Hoyle. At the temperature of the centre of the sun, helium is produced by a series of reactions involving hydrogen and its isotopes. In hotter stars, elements such as carbon and oxygen can form by the uniting of helium nuclei; and, at about a thousand million degrees, these fusion reactions can take the synthesis of matter as far as iron and its neighbours. Beyond this point there is a more fundamental difficulty, because the larger nuclei are less stable. Possibly the heavy elements were formed from stellar explosions (supernovae) which shot high-speed nuclear particles out into space where they met and penetrated other nuclei.

Granular Energy and Radiation

Bolstered by modern discoveries, we find it easy to accept the atomicity of matter. But nature has proved much more radical than this. There is atomicity even in energy and radiation! Of course, in Newton's day it was thought that a beam of light might be a stream of small particles, but this idea was swept away by the triumphs of the wave theory in the 19th century. As this century closed, however, Planck puzzled over the colour of the light radiated from hot bodies.

He could understand the increase of brightness, in going from low to medium frequencies, in terms of the sheer numbers of opportunities for waves in the various bands of frequency. But why did the intensity fall right off at high frequencies where there were even more opportunities? And why did this cut-off gradually move to higher frequencies as the temperature was raised, so changing the colour of the radiation from cherry red to electric blue?

After much difficulty he found himself forced to the revolutionary conclusion that the energy of the radiation is produced in standard lumps – called *quanta* — and that the amount in a lump is proportional to the frequency. This brings in the 'energy millionaire' effect again. For high frequency radiation, big energy quanta are needed and the chance of enough energy gathering together in one pulse for this, in a chaotic assembly of low-temperature heat, is extremely small.

Planck's discovery quickly solved several other problems. Einstein showed that it explained, for example, why the capacities of atoms, molecules and crystals for storing heat are smaller, at low temperatures, than might be expected from the number of elementary particles in them. If the protons and neutrons in a nucleus are jigging about, as also are the electrons in the surrounding atom, why do not all these particles absorb their share of heat? If they did, it would require far more energy to heat a given number of atoms of, say, argon than of helium, whereas in fact there is practically no difference, both sets of atoms responding to heat as if they were *single* particles. The reason is that the elementary constituents of atoms move to and fro at such high frequencies that their energy quanta are much too big for such temperatures. The same applies to the atoms themselves, as constituents of molecules and crystals, at low temperatures.

Einstein also made a striking extension of Planck's idea to the *photo-electric effect*. It was known that metals such as zinc could be provoked into emitting electrons by shining ultraviolet light on them. The high frequency was vital. Strong visible light produced nothing. Einstein realised that this was a quantum effect; that a certain minimum energy has to be supplied to an electron, to enable it to jump out of the metal, and only a high-frequency quantum contains the concentrated energy sufficient for this. No amount of buffeting the metal with low-frequency quanta could make up for an absence of high-frequency ones; it was like hitting the metal with snowballs instead of bullets. In explaining the photo-electric effect Einstein went beyond Planck, for he had shown that the quanta of radiation energy hold together coherently, like particles, as they travel through space, since otherwise it would be impossible for such a quantum to deliver its concentrated blow, when knocking an electron out of the metal. Even light, then, seems to consist of particles (of zero rest-mass) which are called *photons*.

In one sense, this is very familiar. If we sit in bright sunlight we quickly become sunburnt. But if we sit instead, all day, in front of a coal or log fire we may get hot and uncomfortable but only that! The high-frequency ultra-violet component of sunlight, necessary for sunburn, is missing. We can even roughly estimate *Planck's constant*, which connects the energy of the quantum to the frequency, from this, because the typical sunburning process involves knocking an electron out of a molecule in our skin, which means moving it through a potential of a few volts. In fact, the energy quantum of ultra-violet light, with frequency of 1500 million million cycles per second, is roughly about 6 electron-volts. (By comparison, 1 joule is about 6 million million million electron-volts.) We have thus found one of nature's most fundamental constants, which determines the unit of currency in all elementary processes, by sitting in the sun!

7

To the Strange World

The End of the Clockwork Universe

How are we to understand the strange things uncovered in the last chapter? That radiation, which rolls smoothly through space like waves on a calm sea, also jabs at matter like sharp needles? Or the marvellous *stability* of matter: that the atoms of, say, hydrogen are all exactly the same, down to the finest detail of their spectral 'fingerprints', and stay always the same; that salt always crystallises in the same crystals; that pure gold is always characteristically itself; or water? What keeps things as they are? And what are we to make of the chemical forces between atoms, which, in their preferences, exclusiveness, and saturatability, are more like *appetites* than physical forces such as gravitation and electromagnetism?

But there is worse to come. Take two radium atoms, side by side. One of them explodes at 9.30 a.m. on 1 April; the other does not and shows no signs of doing so. How can identical things in identical circumstances behave differently? Moreover, although we can say with great confidence that half of any large number of radium atoms will blow up during the next 1600 years, we never know which particular atom will be the next to go, or when, and it seems that nature does not 'know', either. The radioactive laws are *statistical*, like the insurance company's tables of life expectancy. They are very different from deterministic laws, such as Newton's laws of motion. They are in fact, precisely, those laws of life expectancy for a population, each member of which always has the same chance of dying on the next day, whatever his age.

Of course, statistical laws of nature are familiar from the 19th century, when people worked out the properties of gases from what the molecules were doing *on average*, to avoid the practical difficulty of trying to keep track of all the individuals. But in these problems it was supposed that the individual motions could always be followed *in principle*. The effects now facing us go much deeper. We *can* look at single radioactive atoms, and measure them in all sorts of ways, but this brings us no nearer to knowing when the next will blow up. It is no longer we who are being statistical, *but nature itself*. We have no option but to describe these events statistically, for that is their own nature.

Laplace once championed a deterministic philosophy with the ringing words: 'an intelligence which at a given moment knew all the forces that animate nature, and the respective positions of the beings that compose it, could condense into a single formula the movement of the greatest bodies of the universe and that of the least atom: for such an intelligence nothing could be uncertain, and past and future would be before its eyes'. This grand doctrine is now destroyed by the discovery that nature is uncertain in its most fundamental processes. The 18th century clockwork universe, running absolutely precisely along a single, unambiguous, track from past to future, is swept right away and replaced by a world strangely uncertain.

Scatter Patterns

Nature is indeterministic, but not totally capricious. The latitude in its elementary processes is miniscule compared with the rough clumsiness of even the most skilled watchmaker. And large numbers of the same particles going through the same situation, taken as a whole, behave perfectly regularly and reproducibly in the way they scatter their individual performances over the range open to them. Moreover, this regularity is of a very familiar kind; they sprinkle themselves into patterns of *waves*.

To see how remarkable this is, consider the famous 'two-slit' experiment. First, take a screen with one narrow slit in it. An electron, say, or a photon, is shot at the screen, towards the slit. It passes through and goes on, some way beyond, to hit a photographic film. It makes a mark at one point on the film, like a minute bullet. The mark may not necessarily lie directly opposite the 'gun' since the particle may have been deflected when going through the slit. We repeat this same experiment over and over again, sending electrons through one at a time, all with the same speed, or photons all with the same frequency, and so build up a dense scatter pattern of their marks on the film.

We now cut a second slit in the screen, alongside the first and very close to it. Single electrons are sent through the slits, as before, to make their individual marks on the film, and again we build up a full scatter pattern on a film. What would we expect of this pattern? That it would be simply two overlapping 'one-slit' patterns, each slightly to one side? It is, in fact, quite different, if the slits are really fine and close. It is a set of alternating parallel *bands*; densely marked ones where many electrons struck the film, separated by clear ones where few struck. This is quite incomprehensible in terms of 'ordinary' particles. For how can the *opening* of a second slit *stop* electrons going to where they went quite often in the one-slit experiment? But it is quite simple in terms of waves. When a wave comes through a slit in a screen it spreads out in widening circles of ripples on the other side, as we see on the water behind a narrow opening into a harbour. If there are two such slits, the sets of circular ripples, one from each, overlap; and so along some lines radiating from the slits, where the two sets fit, crest to crest, extra high waves are formed; and between these lie other

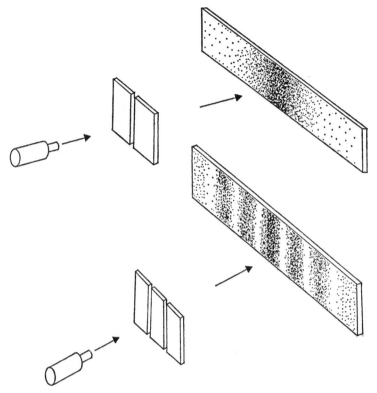

Electrons are fired, one at a time, through fine slits towards a screen, where they are recorded as scatter patterns of black dots. The pattern from a double slit consists of alternating bands, which cannot be reproduced by superimposing two patterns from a single slit. Hence the course of an electron is influenced by both slits in the double slit experiment.

lines along which the waves cancel, crest against trough, leaving the water unmarked. This is just the interference or diffraction of chapter 2 again.

But we seem to be faced with incomprehensibility both ways. If the electrons or photons are 'ordinary' particles, the point marks on the film are understandable, but their sprinkling into alternate bands seems incredible. If they are 'ordinary' waves, the bands are a straightforward diffraction pattern, but the point marks are then incomprehensible.

What such experiments have uncovered is that the most elementary things in nature are neither pure particles nor pure waves, as we have traditionally pictured these out of our ordinary experience. They are something beyond our powers of visual imagination, having both the concentrated 'point-like' qualities of pure particles and the spread-out qualities of pure waves. It is only our *visual* imagination that fails, however; they can be described perfectly well, in mathematical language.

The wave picture obviously comes into its own for the overall behaviour of large numbers of particles, which are congregated where the waves are strong and sparse where the waves are weak. For the single particle going through, however, it tells us little. We cannot say where its mark will be made, only the *likelihood* of its being in one place rather than another. In this sense, the waves are not 'real' at all; they are man-made statistical diagrams, descriptions of the scatter patterns, from which we can read off *probabilities* of individual things happening. But yet, their shapes are firmly governed by the configuration of the apparatus, the arrangement of the slits, etc.; and the fitting of crest to crest and the clashing of crest against trough is equally firmly related to the very real pattern of bands recorded on the film.

Limits to Knowledge

At the heart of all this is the fact that nature always acts in standard amounts. Its 'atom' of activity is Planck's *quantum of action*. Action is a curiously complicated quantity to bear such a fundamental role in nature: it is *mass* multiplied by *length squared* and divided by *time*. Its very complexity suggests that science may have made a wrong turning when it chose to put *mass* on the same level as length and time, as one of the basic ingredients of nature; it would have been simpler to have chosen *energy*, instead, and simpler still to have used a kinematic property such as the Schwartzchild radius, or a characteristic frequency, to measure the substance of things.

Being a conglomerate of several quantities, action can be written in various ways: as mass multiplied by kinematic factors (position multiplied by velocity); as momentum multiplied by length; or as energy multiplied by time. It is useful to look at Planck's constant split up in these various ways. The simplest split is between mass and the kinematic factors. The mass of say a billiard ball is so huge, by the standards here considered, that the kinematic factors such as position and velocity of the ball can be narrowed down – without going to less than one quantum – to far closer limits than we could ever measure in practice. But it is quite otherwise for the electron, with its small mass, which is why the wave effects are so pronounced in this case – although they can be obtained also from neutrons, protons, atoms and molecules, and in principle exist even for billiard balls. Because of its small mass, an electron cannot have a sharply defined velocity without at the same time having a very coarsely defined position, which means, remarkably, that it must then exhibit the consequences of, in effect, being spread over a wide region of space, covering for example all the slits of a diffraction grating.

Another important split is between length and momentum. If we interpret this length as *wavelength* we get *de Broglie's relation* which says that the wavelength to use in the wave analysis of a scatter pattern is Planck's constant divided by the momentum of the particle. A short wavelength implies a big momentum and vice versa. This opens a way to analyse atomic problems systematically. The general method is to work out the wave pattern for the problem in question, by applying the mathematical wave laws, which in this case go by the name of *Schrödinger's equation*. Knowing then the strength and wavelength of the waves at various places in the pattern, the average behaviour of the particles can be deduced.

The quantum of action may be compared to an indivisible lump of soft putty. Squeeze it one way, to make one quantity small, and it spreads out sideways, to make another large. This is important when we make measurements, for a measurement is itself a natural process, subject to the same laws of nature. To measure, say, the position of an electron very precisely we must use an apparatus in which, in effect, length is graduated in very fine units. This is possible only if the contrivance is one that 'squeezes the putty' very thin in the direction of this length. But the putty then inevitably spreads out along the *complementary* direction, which in this case represents momentum, so that our precise measurement of position must make the momentum of the electron very various. We thus find a general limitation in all measurements – and indeed in all physical processes – that exactitude in one quantity inevitably means roughness in its complementary quantity. And it is not merely a roughness in our knowledge of this quantity, but a real roughness in nature itself. The electron trapped in a narrow box, to give it a rather precise position, really does spread itself over a range of momentum, as we can tell for example from its pressure on the walls of the box. Similarly, an electron with a precise velocity has a position spread out over an entire diffraction grating, again with very real consequences.

The analysis of all particular methods of measurement confirms this general conclusion. For example, to fix its position precisely we might try illuminating the electron with an extremely compact photon. But, being so compact, this photon must have a high frequency and hence a big energy and momentum which enables it to thump the electron hard, when they meet, and upset its momentum profoundly.

All this comes from two things. First, from the *universality* of Planck's quantum; nature always acts in steps and because we can work only through natural processes, we cannot be more delicate in measurement than these steps allow. Second, from the *structure* of the quantum, which allows it to be split into complementary pairs of quantities, one of which can be made precise, but only at the cost of roughness in the other. This underlies Heisenberg's *uncertainty* or *indeterminacy principle*, and Bohr's *complementarity principle*. Bohr has also pointed out that one member of each complementary pair is a particle-like property such as energy or momentum, whereas the other is a wave-like property such as frequency or wavelength. A good measurement shapes the putty one way or the other, to emphasise either the particle or the wave aspect of the thing being examined. We cannot tell which slit an electron goes through, in the two-slit experiment, because the apparatus shapes the putty to give a well-defined wave pattern, which leaves the localisation of the electron, as a particle, very ill-defined. To find which slit is used we would have to alter the experiment, for example by illuminating the electron with high-frequency photons, as it goes through, but this change would squeeze the putty differently and destroy the wave pattern producing the diffraction bands.

We come then to the fact that a subjective element is embedded in our pictures of nature at this most fundamental level, because Planck's constant gives us a choice of which aspect we want to have sharply focused and which we are prepared to let be smeared out, when we look at nature. A beam of light or of electrons is one of *neither* waves *nor* particles, in the everyday sense of these words, but of something capable of being squeezed into giving the appearance of either. The very nature of what we see depends on how we look. This conclusion may be disturbing, but it is not altogether unfamiliar. A photograph in a newspaper – is it a coherent picture ('wave' aspect) or a sprinkling of individual dots ('particle' aspect)? It is both, according to our point of view. We find no great difficulty in accepting this particular duality of appearance, or the fact that what we gain from looking at the print depends on how we look at it;

whether we take it all in as a whole, through a general survey, or whether we narrow our sights on to the spotty detail.

How Atoms are Built

The great triumph of the quantum theory is its explanation of the atomic structure. Let us make a hydrogen atom by bringing an electron to a proton. The only sizable force between them is their electrostatic attraction. The electron dances rapidly all round the heavy proton and in a time-lapse photograph the atom would look like a fuzzy round ball of negative electricity centred on a fixed point of positive charge. The ball would be quite large at first but would shrink down as the electron radiated away its energy. But not right down. It would become fixed in size and cease radiating when its diameter was reduced to about one angstrom.

This is a quantum effect. When the electron is confined to a space only one angstrom across, its momentum and hence kinetic energy cannot be *too* small, because of the limit set by the quantum of action. The electron in fact can never be at rest; even at zero temperature it has this 'zero-point motion'. There are thus two energies which act on the atom in opposite directions: its potential energy from the electro-static force, which tries to shrink the ball; and its kinetic energy of 'localisation', from the quantum effect, which tries to expand the ball. A balance is struck and a minimum total energy achieved when the ball is about one angstrom across. The electron is said then to be in a 'stationary state' of motion in the atom, stationary because it does not spon-taneously change with time since every such change could only increase the energy of the atom.

This particular stationary state is the *ground state*, in which the atom is most stable. There are various other states, which can be calculated from Schrödinger's equation, in the form of various kinds of *standing waves*, analogous to those in a steadily blown organ pipe, for example, or to the steady hump of a standing wave of water flowing smoothly over a weir. The 'hump' wave for the ground state of the hydrogen atom is a round ball, dense near the nucleus and thinning out gradually towards the outside. The density of this wave at any point in the ball, when *squared*, gives the portion of time that the electron spends at that point, which is what we would record in our time-lapse photography. The square comes in because waves generally have crests (positive) and troughs (negative), but the portion of time spent can only be positive.

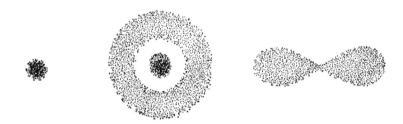

Examples of spherical and dumb-bell shaped electron distributions in an atom. The density of shading indicates roughly the amount of time an electron spends in that region round the atomic nucleus, which is at the centre of the distribution.

The atom can also be quite stable in certain other states. In these 'excited' states the electron has higher energy and spends more time far out from the centre. It is tending towards ionisation. Some of these states look like concentric hollow balls, with a central core. Others look like dumb-bells, two equal globules symmetrically placed on either side of the nucleus between them. Three different dumb-bell states exist at the same energy, at right angles along three axes through the nucleus. States of more complicated shape occur at still higher energies.

When the atom is in an excited state, or is struck by

another particle, its wave pattern may suddenly flick over
to another one, of different energy, rather as a badly played
wind instrument squeaks by suddenly jumping into a different
state of vibration. The change in energy is made up by the
atom giving out or taking in, as the case may be, a photon
of the right frequency. This is how sharp atomic spectrum
lines are made.

The electron clouds of other atoms are much like those of
hydrogen, but pulled in more tightly by the stronger nuclear
attraction. The two electrons in helium, for example, are
held in a much smaller ground-state ball and the ionisation
energy to get one of them out of this is nearly twice that of
hydrogen. Does this mean that the heavier atoms are smaller
still? No, because nature applies another quantum restriction, summarised in Pauli's *exclusion principle* that, when
several electrons exist together, only two of them (which
must have 'opposite spins') can share each single wave
pattern. The spin is a property of the electron, in some ways
like the spin of the earth round its polar axis, and it produces magnetic effects from which the magnetism of iron is
derived. In a magnetic field the electron sets its spin axis
either 'up' or 'down' the direction of the field; these are its
two opposite spins.

After helium, the next element is lithium. It has three
electrons, only two of which can share the basic round ball
state. The third has to go into one of higher energy, well out
in the suburbs of the atom, where it is largely shielded from
the nucleus by the other two, close to the centre. It can thus
fairly easily escape altogether, leaving a positive ion behind.
This easy ionisation is the classic feature of a *metal*.

A striking feature of many heavier atoms is the 'closed
shell' of eight electrons. This comes from four types of
electron cloud, one ball-shaped and three dumb-bell,
which all occur at about the same level of energy, each of
which can take two electrons of opposite spins. The eight
electrons in such a 'shell' jointly form a full round ball of

electrical charge. They are all quite strongly held in the atom because none is heavily shielded from the nucleus by the others. As a result, atoms whose outermost shells are of this 'closed' type have little incentive to join up with others to form molecules. Why should they, when their electron clouds are beautifully complete and symmetrical, with every electron enjoying a strong electrostatic force from its own nucleus? The atoms with this 'satisfied' electronic structure are, together with helium, the *inert gas* series of elements.

Chemically reactive atoms have unsatisfied electronic structures; they have either too many or not enough electrons to make closed outer shells; and their 'ambition' is to get such shells by joining up with other atoms so that they can give away or pick up the necessary electrons. The *electropositive* or *electron-donor* atoms that give away one or a few electrons, surplus to their closed-shell needs, are mainly the metals. The *electronegative* or *electron-acceptor* atoms which have some electron 'holes' in their outer shells, hungry for extra electrons, are found in substances such as oxygen, sulphur, chlorine and fluorine.

More Particles

In 1932 the physical world seemed reduced to four basic particles – electrons, protons, neutrons, and photons – variously arranged in huge numbers. It soon became complicated again. The seeds for this were planted four years earlier by Dirac, who set out to make quantum theory consistent with special relativity, i.e. independent of the speed of the observer. An immediate outcome was that some new features turned up in the quantum laws, which implied that particles such as electrons and protons carried the properties of 'spin'.

This was a great triumph but there was also a problem. Because of its affinity with Pythagoras's theorem, the special theory of relativity is full of square roots. In Dirac's case it produced the square root of *energy*. But a square root can be positive or negative. What then is a *negative* energy? It seemed to suggest a particle going *backwards* in time! In 1931 Dirac solved this enigma by showing that the negative sign could be transferred from energy, where it made no sense, to the electrical charge, where it converted the already negative electron into a *positive* one. He had thus predicted what is now called the *positron*, an 'anti-particle' identical with the electron in every way except for its opposite charge.

The positron was actually observed in 1932. Under certain conditions, such as by collision with a nucleus, powerful gamma-ray photons can turn into *pairs* of electrons and positrons. The process is reversible; if these opposite particles subsequently come together they annihilate in a flash of gamma photons. Subsequently, other anti-particles were found, appearing in pairs in which a conserved property such as electrical charge is created in equal and opposite amounts. Anti-protons were produced in 1955. When these pass very close to protons, it is sometimes possible for the opposite charges to cancel in such a way as to leave behind two *neutral* particles, one a neutron, the other an anti-neutron, with an opposite magnetic field.

Recent experiments have suggested that the spin and magnetic properties of these uncharged particles may be due to charged 'sub-particles' moving about inside them. We have gone from atoms to nuclei, nuclei to nuclear particles, and now find a hint of yet another layer of granularity within these supposedly elementary particles! Is there no end to nature's 'wheels within wheels'?

The discovery of anti-matter is satisfying in showing a basic symmetry in nature. But why, at least in our part of the universe, is the positive charge commonly in protons, and the negative in electrons? One possibility is that there may be similarly large amounts of anti-matter, separated far away from us, in 'anti-galaxies'. It is not obvious how we would recognise this, because the 'anti-photons' they could send are just the same as ordinary photons; but of course, a galaxy and anti-galaxy colliding and mutually annihilating would make a fine sight.

A common type of nuclear radioactivity is *beta-decay* in which a neutron turns into a proton, or vice versa, and an electron or positron is created, to conserve charge, and spat out of the nucleus. Pauli first realised that, to conserve energy and momentum in this, another particle had to be created as well; and this theory of the *neutrino* was then worked out convincingly by Fermi, in 1934. Neutrinos and anti-neutrinos are plentiful – huge numbers pass through our bodies all the time – but cannot be felt because they have no charge and no rest-mass (and so move at the speed of light). They spin, however, as if spiralling along invisible screw threads through space, the neutrino always spiralling one way round and the anti-neutrino the other way. They can go right through the earth with almost no chance of a collision, but nevertheless were detected in 1956. More recently, slightly different kinds of neutrinos have also been found in decay processes involving yet another kind of particle, the *muon*, which seems to be an excited and unstable version of the electron, 207 times heavier than the ordinary one.

Beta-decay produced other surprises. In early 1957, Madame Wu, at the suggestion of Lee and Yang, studied the spinning nuclei of radioactive cobalt, which act as magnets. By cooling them severely in a strong magnetic field she made many of them line up their magnetic axes together; and found from this, that in beta-decay, they shot out more electrons from their *south* poles than the north. This discovery of a lop-sidedness in nature, which goes by the name of 'failure of conservation of parity', came as a tremendous shock. There is an *absolute* difference between the north and south end of such a nucleus; nature is *not* symmetrical in this! It was so surprising that in fact, with hindsight, people realised that the effect had been seen many years earlier but put on one side as an unbelievable oddity and forgotten.

By nuclear standards, beta-decay is a slow process, without much push behind it. It must be due in fact to something, called the *weak force*, quite different from the strong force that holds nuclei together. In all of nature there appear to be only *four* fundamental forces. From the strongest to the weakest they are: strong nuclear; electromagnetic; weak nuclear; and gravitational. Together they push and pull the whole universe – everything – along its course of destiny.

But what are forces, anyway? The extraordinary answer now is: they are particles! As a start, let us recall that the photon and the electrical force between charges are two aspects of the same general thing, electromagnetism. We also recall that energy and time are shackled together as complementary quantities in the quantum of action. This means that nature allows energy to fluctuate upwards, temporarily breaking the law of conservation of energy, provided that things get back to normal again in a time, within the uncertainty principle, too short to be detectable. As a result, when for example one electron is near another, it can send a photon to be absorbed by the other, provided that the energy and lifetime of this photon fall within the quantum allowance. Such transfers of transient photons, called *virtual* particles, deflect the electrons and we recognise this as the effect of the 'inverse-square electrical force' between them.

Yukawa in 1935 extended this idea to the strong nuclear force. A big difference here is that this force has a much shorter range than the electrical one. Yukawa saw that this implied a very short time in the uncertainty relation; and hence a large energy for the virtual particle, which had to be regarded as the Einstein energy of the *rest-mass* of a particle reckoned to be about 300 times as heavy as an electron. These *pi-meson* or *pion* particles are of course virtual ones, living within the internal world of nuclear forces, but, by hitting nuclei very hard with protons, they can be driven out into the external world as real particles.

In this modern view, particles are no longer acted on by invisible, continuous and mysterious 'fields of force'. The only events in their lives are collisions with other particles, virtual or real. Except for these, their world is a void. This is the ultimate granularity of nature! Whether even gravitation is granular remains an open question. There are reasons for believing that gravitational waves might exist and might even be quantised as *graviton* particles, but their detection is fantastically difficult.

Over the last 30 years many unstable particles heavier than protons have been realised. They seem to be excited relatives – with high internal energy – of the same general family as protons and neutrons. There are also clear indications of internal structures in the proton and neutron, and people have speculated that some fundamentally new particles, *quarks* or *partons*, may be found there.

The situation with all these many and different particles is rather like that in chemistry in the 19th century, when the atoms of the chemical elements were known but not understood. Indeed, a set of rules has now been discovered which, like Mendeleev's periodic table, arranges the particles in such orderly and systematic patterns that it must certainly have a deeper significance. It has, for example, been used successfully to predict the existence of new unstable particles from gaps in the patterns.

An important feature of these new unstable particles is their *heaviness*. Quarks, if they exist, may even be heavier than the proton or neutron which they compose. The parts are greater than the whole! This is of course because, when such parts come together, so much energy is radiated away from them that the remaining internal energy, and with it the mass of the whole composed particle, is greatly diminished. In this sense, we have reached the *end* of our search for the elements of nature. The smallest things which have rest-mass are the electron; and also the proton, neutron, and the mesons which commute between them. The heavier particles are not so much discovered as *made*, by pumping large amounts of energy into existing particles through high-speed collisions. Again, we have to remember the uncertainty relation here. A sub-particle localised within the diameter of a proton (about one-quarter of a million-millionth of a centimetre) would, because of Planck's constant, have a momentum equivalent to an energy far greater than an electron; and, if we go to much smaller diameters than this, the energy and rest-mass of the sub-particle rise beyond those of all known particles. As Brillouin has emphasised, this also sets a *practical* limit to the idea of space and time continuous down to infinitesimal sizes.

Bits of Information

In the two-slit experiment we destroyed the coherent pattern of interfering waves when we located the electron at one of the slits by hitting it with a photon. The collision is an *irreversible* change for that electron. Every measurement is an irreversible process which transfers some *information* from the object of study to the recording instrument – as for example when an electron blackens a grain in a photographic plate, or a motor-car sends back a reflected radar pulse in a speed trap – and we can begin to think of even *information* itself as a tangible commodity, shunted about in natural processes.

The theory of this is due mainly to Shannon and Brillouin. The 'atom' of information is the *bit*, which is an answer to a single yes-no question. A good television picture provides about 100 million bits of information per second. The thing measured by bits is *position*. This may actually be position as such, for example the position of a particle along a line or a car in a car park, or it may be a 'position' which stands for something else, for example time indicated by the hands of a clock, or speed by the pointer on a speedometer dial, or a

letter by a child's finger running along the written alphabet.
The *amount of information* is the *number of bits* needed to give
the position. For example, referring to a chess-board, a
statement such as 'white king four' in the language of the
game picks out one particular square and in so doing conveys
6 bits of information, as follows. There are 64 squares in all
so that this is the spread of our initial ignorance. One
yes-no answer to an efficient question (e.g. 'is the square in
this half of the board?') brings it down to 32; a second to
16; and so on, so that we can locate one particular square
by 6 such answers.

In physical problems the amount of information, multiplied by a conversion constant, is known as *negative entropy*
or *negentropy*, because of its close relation to a property called
entropy which measures the spread of possible arrangements
open to a physical system. For example, a 'crystal' of 32
'white' atoms and 32 'black' ones, laid out like the white and
black squares of the chessboard, would have only this one
arrangement available in this *ordered* state. But if it were
allowed to become *disordered*, by random rearrangement of
these atoms among the white and black squares, 64 bits of
information (or, more exactly, 63 because there is no choice
for the last square) would be needed to identify which, out
of all the possible arrangements, the crystal was then using
at any particular instant; the 'configurational entropy' of
the crystal is, in different units, a measure of this 64 bits.

The conversion factor, to the thermodynamic units in
which entropy and negentropy are usually measured, is
such that one million million million million bits is about
10 joules per degree of absolute temperature. A bit of information is small by everyday standards, but not by those
of elementary processes, and we see in the thermodynamic
units of this conversion factor something of the physical
reality of information. In the words of Gabor, 'you can never
get something for nothing, not even an observation'.

8

To the Familiar World

Sticking Together

The familiar world of everyday things all round us, even ourselves, is made of huge numbers of atoms sticking together in clumps of various sizes and shapes. How is this done? In the end it is all due to the simple electrostatic attraction between opposite charges, but this comes in various heavily disguised forms. Well away from a neutral atom, the positive and negative forces due to its nucleus and electrons cancel each other so exactly that the net force from them, the 'chemical' force, is zero there. And so chemical forces are 'short-range' ones, even though they come from the long-range electrostatic force.

Near to the atom, however, its granular structure begins to play a part, because it enables an approaching particle to get closer to some charges in the atom than others, particularly when these charges alter their positions slightly. As a result, the particle can come under the sway of electrical forces which are no longer so precisely balanced, positive against negative. The first intimation of these short-range effects is a rather weak attraction, called the *van der Waals force*, which all atoms feel towards one another while still a little way apart.

But for the real chemical forces we must look to 'reactive' atoms at close quarters, where the outer suburbs of their electron clouds actually overlap. In a single atom of this kind these outer electrons are not ideally arranged. They *cannot* be, in the neutral atom, because the number of them needed to balance the charge of the nucleus is different from that needed to give the best 'shell' structure from the energy point of view. There are either too many for this, or not quite enough. As a result, such an atom has the possibility of reducing its energy by getting close to other atoms in such a way as to improve its outer shell structure. This is what holds us all together. The simplest example is the *ionic bond*, as in common salt. In this, a sodium atom gives up its outermost 'valency' electron, which is easily ionised, to a chlorine atom where it fills up the single 'electron-hole' in the outermost electron cloud. In this way both atoms achieve those 'closed-shell' structures which we know, from the inert gases, to be most satisfactory types of electron cloud. But in so doing, both have become *ions*. The sodium, having lost one electron, is now a positive one; and the chlorine similarly is negative. And so they cling together electrostatically.

This is quite a strong bond. It makes salt crystals fairly hard and stops them melting until red-hot. But the electrostatic force between two atoms goes up as the *square* of the number of electrons given by the one to the other; and so we find great strengths and high melting points in the *ceramic* oxides of magnesium, calcium, aluminium and titanium, which include such substances as sapphire, ruby, emerald and lime (immortalised in the 'limelight' of Victorian illuminations).

In all such crystals the ions are laid out in patterns of alternate positive and negative charges. In the simplest ones the patterns are cubic, as can be seen from the shapes of salt crystals, but there are many more complicated structures as in the silicates (e.g. clays), carbonates (e.g. marble, chalk), nitrates (e.g. saltpetre) and sulphates (e.g. gypsum, plaster of paris) in which one of the ions is a molecule. Some substances crystallise in *layers*, held together by weak forces.

They can be flaky (e.g. mica), soft (e.g. talc) or slippery (e.g. hydroxides, soap flakes).

Because of its special structure of one electron in a shell made for only two, a hydrogen atom can go either way in an ionic compound. It can be a negative partner, taking an electron from, say, lithium or calcium; or it can be a positive partner, giving an electron to, say, fluorine or oxygen. It is never a *full* donor, however, because the bare proton is too attractive to electrons to allow that. But even as a partial donor, with a little of the electron cloud still clinging to it, an electropositive hydrogen atom in a molecule can be attractive enough to the negative parts of other molecules to enable weak *hydrogen bonds* to form between them. These hold many biological molecules together.

In a molecule of water, the two hydrogen atoms are embedded into the ends of two half-empty 'dumb-bell' electron clouds which stick out at right-angles in the oxygen atom. The hydrogens force this angle apart by several more degrees, so that the molecule looks rather like a dog's hind leg, with the oxygen at the bend and the hydrogens at the ends. It is the basis of several unique features of water, such as the complex structures of ice crystals, the exquisite patterns of snow flakes, the expansion on freezing which bursts water pipes, splits rocks and breaks up winter soils, and the melting of ice under pressure which helps the skater along.

Its ionic nature is particularly important in enabling water to intermingle with soils and clays, and to wet non-greasy surfaces. Water also dissolves salts easily, because it allows their ions to separate, being shielded from one another's electrostatic forces by the 'polarisation' of its intervening molecules, which turn their positive hydrogen ends towards the negative ions and their oxygen centres towards the positive ions. In fact, even water itself slightly dissociates, to make a dilute solution of positive hydrogen ions and negative 'hydroxyl' ones (one oxygen plus one hydrogen atom). Pure water has equal numbers of both, but when an *acid* is added, which is a source of hydrogen ions, the concentration of these goes up and that of hydroxyl ions goes down. The reverse happens when an *alkali* or *base* is added to water, for this is a source of hydroxyl ions. Acidity is measured by the well-known 'pH' value, which ranges from about 1 for strong acids, such as concentrated sulphuric, to 7 for pure water and neutral salt solutions, and up to 14 for strong alkalis, such as concentrated caustic soda. Many acids or alkalis are made by the combination of an oxide with water. Sandy soils owe their acidity to the silica (silicon oxide) in them, and alkaline soils to their chalk or lime content (calcium and magnesium oxides).

What happens when *two* protons compete for a single electron? Their struggle is resolved by the electron cloud of the ground state spreading itself, roughly in the shape of an ellipse, equally between the two of them, so that when they are really close the electron is able to spend most of its time in the space between them and hold them together as a hydrogen molecule in the form of a positive ion. However, Pauli's principle permits *two* electrons of opposite spins in such a wave pattern, and so a neutral *hydrogen molecule* can in this way be formed between two hydrogen atoms. This is an example of the *covalent bond*.

It is in this bond that we meet the saturation of chemical forces. Suppose that a third hydrogen atom comes up to this covalently bonded pair. The electron cloud of the ground state could in principle spread between all three. But only two electrons would be allowed in it and the third would have to go into a state of higher energy. This makes the three-atom hydrogen molecule unstable and it does not normally exist. The same limitation applies to many other covalent atom-pair molecules, which exist as gases at room temperature.

The carbon atom makes innumerable covalent compounds, because its four electrons and four electron-holes in its outer shell provide plenty of opportunities for forming covalent bonds by sharing electrons, in pairs, with other atoms. It produces in *diamond* the ideal covalent crystal, in which each carbon atom links up with four carbon atom neighbours by sharing two electrons with each. The four covalent bonds stick out symmetrically from the carbon atom, along the four diagonal directions between opposite corners of a cube, so that the pattern of atoms in diamond has a cubic basis.

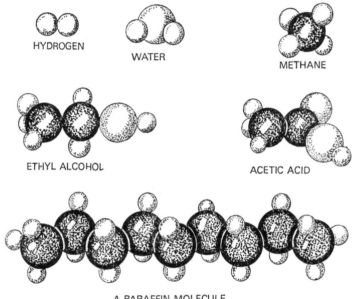

HYDROGEN

WATER

METHANE

ETHYL ALCOHOL

ACETIC ACID

A PARAFFIN MOLECULE

Some simple molecules. The small atoms are hydrogen, the large light ones are oxygen and the large dark ones are carbon.

The many 'organic' compounds which carbon makes with hydrogen, oxygen, and other substances, include the very stuff of life itself. The simplest is the methane molecule, four hydrogen atoms on the four covalent bonds of the carbon atom. Endless variations are possible by taking one or more of these hydrogens away and putting other things in their place, including the joining of two or more such molecules into larger ones. Replacement of a hydrogen atom by a hydroxyl molecule gives an *alcohol*. Its replacement by a *carboxyl* group (carbon-oxygen-oxygen-hydrogen) gives an *organic acid* such as vinegar. Replacement of several in the larger hydrocarbon molecules by a certain number of oxygens gives the *carbohydrates* or *sugars*, in which the proportions of hydrogen and oxygen atoms are the same as in water. In the larger molecules the carbon atoms may be joined up into rings, as in *benzene* and *turpentine*, or into open chains as in the *paraffins*.

A *polymer* is a long-chain compound having a backbone of hundreds or thousands of atoms or molecules joined one to the next, like a line of beads, with other atoms or molecules stuck on the side to mop up the remaining bonds. In many organic polymers the backbone is a line of carbon atoms. The simplest is *polyethylene*, a familiar household 'plastic', in which two hydrogen atoms are attached to each carbon atom along the chain. In other familiar substances such as *vinyl*, *polystyrene* and *perspex*, some of the hydrogens are replaced by other atoms or molecules. When these side molecules possess linking bonds also at their outer ends, they may connect one polymer chain to another, so *cross-linking* them into a network, as in *bakelite* and other solid plastics. In polymers such as *natural rubber*, *cellulose* and *nylon*, other atoms and molecules besides carbon are also built into the backbone itself.

At ordinary temperatures polymers without cross-links are often sticky liquids, such as raw rubber as tapped from the tree, their long-chain molecules wriggling and slithering over one another like a heap of earthworms. The weak forces between these saturated molecules are easily overcome by the heat motions at ordinary temperatures. But if the forces are a bit stronger, as in perspex, the convoluted mass remains fairly rigid at room temperature and the substance is a *glassy* solid. Some of the most interesting effects are got by slightly cross-linking the molecules of a sticky liquid polymer, as when raw rubber is 'vulcanised' by putting in a few cross-linking sulphur molecules. A skeleton network of irregular molecular threads is then formed throughout the mass, co-ordinating it weakly into a jelly. The extraordinary elastic flexibility of rubber comes from this. Normally the threads of the network are crumpled up by the random heat motions, but they can be pulled out fairly straight by an applied force, so stretching the rubber enormously. When the force is released the heat motions crumple them up again and the rubber goes back to its original shape.

If a number of similar polymer threads are laid together, straight, side by side, the forces between them, although weak, are nevertheless sometimes sufficient to hold the bundle together as a kind of fibrous 'crystal'. Such materials are often mechanically strong, as we know from nylon, Dacron, Terylene, and other similar man-made fibres. Natural fibres such as cellulose, collagen, silk, gelatin, and keratin, form the sinews of the living world. Wood, cotton, flax, wool, hair, fur, leather, horn, tendon, muscle and gut come from them; and collagen fibres hold together the calcium-bearing constituents in bone.

Oil and water do not mix. This everyday remark reminds us that saturated covalent substances, such as oils, greases and waxes, are not attractive enough to ionic substances to persuade the molecules of these to tear themselves away from one another to open up space for a covalent molecule. However, some organic molecules have ionically 'active' ends, such as hydroxyl or carboxyl units, and can then attach themselves to water or even, as in the familiar case of alcohol, dissolve in it. Soap and detergent molecules consist of hydrocarbon chains, attractive to oil at their covalent ends and, because of a carboxyl or similar group, also attractive to water at their other, ionic, ends. They can thus clean a greasy dish by insinuating themselves along the interface between the grease and glaze, their oily ends towards the grease and ionic ones towards the glaze. Water can penetrate with them, along the ionic interface, and then float off the grease. Similarly, a lump of grease can be broken up into small drops, each coated with a layer of these oriented molecules, which can disperse through the water as an *emulsion*. Again, a *foam* or *froth* is an 'emulsion' of air bubbles mixed in water coated with such molecules, which stabilise it.

The element *silicon*, chemically similar to carbon, plays a part in the mineral world as important as that of carbon in the organic one. Most rocks are silicate minerals. Here also cross-linked chain structures are formed, but in this case the silicon dioxide (silica sand, quartz, granite) molecular unit plays a key role; the silicon atoms are linked to one another, not directly, but via the oxygen atoms. Because of this cross-linking into networks of branching, interconnected, chains of molecules, molten silica and its compounds do not easily crystallise on cooling, but tend instead to solidify into *glasses*, as in quickly chilled basalt from volcanoes (obsidian). Silica, being an acidic oxide, combines with various metal oxides to form silicates, the constituents of most rocks. Man-made glasses and glazes are various fairly pure forms of silicate glass made from silica sand melted up with oxides of sodium, aluminium, calcium and (for Pyrex) boron. Enamels are glazes to which white 'filler' oxides and coloured pigment oxides have been added.

Metals

To understand metals, let us begin with a perfect diamond-like crystal of pure silicon. It is an electrical insulator. This is because the covalent bonds between the atoms are all perfectly filled; every electron is in its place; there are none left over, or electron-holes in the network of covalently bonded atoms. It is like a theatre with all seats full and no standing, or empty seats, allowed. You can still move from seat to seat, but only by changing places with neighbours, which produces no flow or 'current' through the theatre from the entrance to the exit. In just this way the insulator crystal cannot conduct an electrical current, even if its electrons change places inside it.

For conduction, this rigid perfection must be broken down. In the theatrical analogy, standing or empty seats must be allowed. Standing people can then walk right through, to the exit, or drop into seats left empty by previous occupants. If someone near the exit goes out, his empty place can then be 'worked' backwards by other occupants moving up in turn, one by one, until eventually it passes out of the theatre at the entrance, so letting in someone from the queue outside; this is conduction by the movement of 'holes'.

There are several ways in which all this can be brought about: by ionising radiations or high voltage discharges, which knock electrons out of their covalent bonds, rather as the air is made conducting in a lightning stroke; by heat, which can excite some electrons out of their covalent bonds in the 'energy millionaire' effect of chapter 6; and by the presence in the crystal of impurity atoms with the 'wrong' number of electrons for the perfect covalent bond structure. For example, a phosphorous atom can replace a silicon atom in the crystal lattice, but it has *five* outer electrons. There are jobs for four of these, linking up covalently with the silicon atom neighbours, but not for the fifth which remains unemployed, weakly attached, and can be easily ionised off the phosphorous atom to wander freely throughout the whole crystal. Conversely, an impurity atom of lower valency leaves an electron-hole in the covalent bond structure, which again may leave home and wander through the whole crystal. These are the *impurity semi-conductors*, the transistor crystals.

Such imperfections in the electronic structure of a crystal, being negatively or positively charged, are also centres of electrostatic force and energy, which resist ionisation. However, when ionisation is already well advanced, a major new effect sets in which encourages yet more ionisation: the mobile electrons or electron-holes make the crystal too good a conductor to allow long-range electrostatic fields to exist inside it. The 'cloud' of mobile charge spaces itself round any particular one so as to compensate for its charge, rather as the molecules in water enable charged ions to separate, in solution, by shielding them from one another's electrical influences.

Such massive ionisation occurs naturally and spontaneously in metals and their outer electrons remain always free to conduct electricity. The reason is that metals have only a few outer electrons, easily ionisable off their parent atoms and not enough in number to fill up a covalent bond structure. The quantum restrictions which make pure silicon an insulator no longer apply in a metal. Most of the seats in the theatre are empty.

We can thus picture a metal as a crowd of round positive ions immersed in a 'sea' of free electrons, the whole group being held together by the electrical attraction between the positive ions and the negative sea. The free movement of the conducting electrons in this sea accounts also for their silvery reflectivity, because electromagnetic waves cannot pass through a region of freely moving charges. They must be reflected from it.

The fluidity of the electron 'glue', which holds the ions together, is important for several features of metals. It allows the ions to fit together in simple close-packed crystal structures and it tolerates the replacement of one ion by another of a different metal, which enables various metals to mix together freely and interchangeably in *alloys*. The close-packed crystal structures provide smooth planes of atoms which can slide rather easily over each other, being held together at all times by the mobile electron glue. The ability of metals to change shape by *plastic deformation*, with one atomic layer sliding over another, rather than splitting apart as in brittle crystals, originates here.

The atomic layers slide over one another flexibly, a bit at a time. They sit on one another like wrinkled wallpaper and, just as freshly-laid pieces of wallpaper can be slid over their wall by brushing the wrinkles along, so the crystal layers can slide by brushing their wrinkles – called *dislocations* – along the interfaces between them. The analogy continues

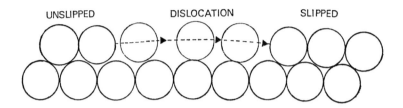

Slip of one crystal layer over another. The front of the upper layer has already slipped forwards by one atomic spacing and this slip process is now working its way towards the back by the backwards movement of the dislocation. The diagram is a side view of the two crystal layers, in which the dislocation forms the boundary line between the slipped and unslipped regions of the layers.

further. A clumsy wall-paperer, trying to rectify his original mistakes, may make things even worse by brushing in still more wrinkles. Similarly, a plastically deforming crystal generally multiplies the dislocation lines in itself; so that when a metal car bumper is crumpled in a collision, millions of dislocations are created in it, in dense tangles. Alloy particles can make a metal hard by getting in the way of the dislocations and holding them up, rather as the wallpaper wrinkles may catch on to bits of grit, on the wall, and remain hung up on them.

Chemistry of the Earth

In a universe of mainly hydrogen and helium, how do we happen to enjoy such a richly diverse chemistry, on earth? The common motion of all the planets and minor bodies around the sun, and the similar ages measured for the earth, moon and meteorites, suggest that the whole solar system grew out of the gravitational contraction of a common cloud of gas and dust, about 4600 million years ago. It is likely that the sun and planets all formed together, but also possible that the sun formed first and then the planets from gas drawn from it.

Only the large outer planets such as Jupiter have kept their original hydrogen and helium, as is shown by their low densities, roughly comparable to that of water. The four inner planets are small, rocky and dense, the average density of the earth being 5.5 times that of water. It is fairly certain from this and other evidence, including the scarcity of gases such as neon in our atmosphere, that most of the original material of the earth has been stripped away, leaving a heavy residue, mainly of iron. We are the remains of a grand alchemical distillation!

Iron, and its companion metals such as nickel, have only a moderate affinity for oxygen. At the high temperatures of the early earth they would have remained chemically un-combined and, because of their density, have sunk mainly to the centre, forming a metal ball, the *core*, which we know – from the pathways of earthquake waves passing through the earth – to have a radius about half that of the earth (6400 km.). The lighter and more reactive elements such as silicon, aluminium, calcium and magnesium, together with some iron, combined with oxygen and one another to form the various silicates and alumino-silicates. These make up the surrounding *mantle* of *magma*, semi-molten rock about 3000 km. thick, and the outer *crust*, the few kilometres thickness of solid ground which, at a density of 2.6, floats on the surface.

The early earth, over 4000 million years ago, would have been a fearsome sight: a red-hot and turbulent ball of molten minerals, belching out vast clouds of gases and steam; pieces of crust solidifying at the surface, cracking and floating apart to allow liquid rock to gush out, under pressure, from the magma inside; remelting and solidifying, over and over again, in the crust's struggle to establish itself over the globe;

gradually consolidating over hundreds of millions of years into a continuous crust, though repeatedly rent with earthquakes and densely pock-marked with volcanoes, spewing out lava, gases and steam. The atmosphere then, quite unlike today's, was a great cloud of water vapour, hydrogen, methane, ammonia, hydrogen sulphide, and other gaseous compounds of hydrogen, oxygen, nitrogen and carbon. The free hydrogen gradually escaped into space, to be partly replaced with hydrogen from water molecules disintegrated by the sun's high-energy photons, this water in turn being replenished from the steam and gases spurting out of the volcanic pores through the crust. The oxygen was consumed by the ammonia, to make water and nitrogen, and by the substances in the crust to make oxides.

Gradually, through the millennia running up to about 3500 million years ago, the crust and atmosphere cooled, and the clouds of water vapour condensed into torrential rain which poured without respite for centuries, wearing down the primordial crust, cutting great canyons, washing the debris down into deposits which consolidated into the first sedimentary rocks; and filling up the lower reaches with water to make the primeval oceans. Although vast in extent, now covering three-quarters of the earth's surface to an average depth of about 4 km., the oceans nevertheless amount to no more than the equivalent of a mere film of dampness on a billiard ball.

Life began in these early oceans, over 3000 million years ago. Hardly more than a 'soup' of organic molecules at first, it then advanced through the grouping together of such molecules into the simplest organisms, the *bacteria* and *algae*. The next great evolutionary step, the ability to make food from the energy of sunlight through the photochemical reaction of *chlorophyll*, the green pigment of plants, also led to the release of oxygen as a by-product, which entered the atmosphere and began gradually to bring it towards its present composition. Going extremely slowly for over 1000 million years, this oxygen-making process did not really take off until life first appeared on land, about 350 million years ago, and the earth entered the *carboniferous* period, over 250 million years ago, when vast swamp forests laid down what have become today's coal beds.

The Last 200 Million Years

The earth of two hundred million years ago would have seemed not entirely strange to us. It was a world of blue skies and clouds, with a variable but on the whole acceptable climate, with green vegetation, with many of today's mountain ranges, such as the Scottish Highlands, the Urals and the Appalachians, and with many kinds of animals, of species extinct today but nevertheless known from their fossilised remains in museums. Geographically, however, it would have been almost unrecognisable. Most of the present sea-floor crust did not exist then. There were no Atlantic, Indian, Arctic or Antarctic oceans. Dating of the sedimentary deposits on these ocean floors – and measurements of magnetic directions in successive stripes of magma rock, which have surged up, molten, through cracks (*rifts*) in these floors and then solidified along the edges of these cracks – have shown that different regions of these floors have been drifting apart, away from a *mid-ocean ridge* which is the site of the rifts and faults.

The first idea of such movements came from *Wegener* who pointed out the striking geographical 'fit' between the east and west coasts bordering the Atlantic ocean, and suggested from this the theory of *continental drift*. Backed up by the recent geological discoveries of the sea-floor movements, this has now developed into the theory of *plate tectonics* which pictures the earth's crust as like an eggshell cracked into seven major plates which float and move about on a viscous foundation. The mid-ocean ridges and rifts are cracks, opening up between plates drifting apart, and filling up with new rock from the interior. Along other cracks, the great plates scrape past one another, producing earthquakes; or butt into one another so that one is forced down into a trench beneath the other; or they crumple and heave up into new mountain masses, again with many earthquakes.

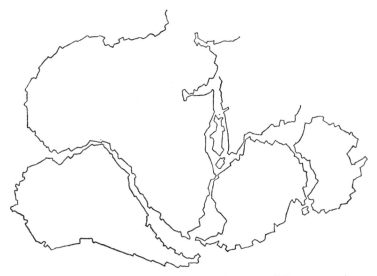

The supercontinent of Gondwanaland, 200 million years ago.

Two hundred million years ago the land mass of the world probably existed as one great continent, *Pangaea,* its southern part named *Gondwanaland.* The cracks developed, forming rift valleys, which split apart and allowed the seas to flood in, between them. The continents have been carried along with the ocean floor on which they sit, like coal on a conveyer belt. One such split took the Americas away from Europe and Africa, and produced the Andes and Rocky mountains where the American plates butted into the Pacific plate. The Himalayan mountains were made about 45 million years ago, by the plate carrying India travelling some 5000 km. northwards, across the now Indian ocean, and crumpling up against the plate carrying Asia.

The edges between plates are the regions where the earth's

ancient physical violence still lingers today. They are the active zones, the sites of earthquakes and volcanoes, such as the border of the Pacific ocean, and the lines running through the Mediterranean and Asia Minor, the sites of new, high and sharp peaks, such as the Himalayas, Alps and the mountains round the Pacific.

The movements of the plates at these boundaries can be measured. The sides of the *San Andreas fault* in California, for example, are 'creeping' past each other at about 5 centimetres a year. Such creep does not usually continue smoothly. Sections of a fault get stuck together and remain locked for years, while the strain piles up against them from the dislocations emanating from nearby creeping sections. Eventually this strain becomes unbearable and a locked section releases all the accumulated deformation, in the sudden large slip of an earthquake. The prediction of earthquakes thus depends on the measurement of creep along faults.

Over the vast reaches of geological time, living matter has had other major effects on the chemistry of the earth, as well as making atmospheric oxygen and laying down fossil fuel deposits. During the *cretaceous period*, some 100 million years ago, the chalky skeletons of innumerable small creatures – mussels, cockles, and especially corals – were laid down in great beds, thickening at about 1 centimetre per 400 years, which have become today's limestone deposits.

Much more recently, during the last one million years, the outstanding geological events have been the recurring *ice ages*, separated by warmer *interglacial periods*, including the one we enjoy today which began about 10,000 years ago. During the ice ages, great glaciers, like those on Greenland or Antarctica, spread down from the polar regions to cover much of Europe, Asia and North America. In Britain they reached as far as the north side of the Thames Valley. They cut great valleys, scoring and grinding the rocks over which they passed, carrying with them great loads of boulder rocks, moraine gravels and boulder clays which they deposited where they rested, melted and retreated; and they left behind many confused mixtures of soils – clays, gravels, sands – swept up during their outward journeys and dropped during their retreats.

The various types of soils, the silica-rich *sands*, the aluminosilicate *clays*, the limestone *chalks*, the organic *peats*, the rich *loams* in which sands, clays and organic *humus* from decayed plants are mixed – all these have been formed by the more recent geological processes. Surface rocks have been shattered to *screes* by frost, finely ground by the rain, rivers, and glaciers, washed together and deposited as sedimentary beds, and then enriched with organics from the debris of countless plants since grown there. In cold climates the silicates of iron and other metals tend to be washed away rather more than the quartz silica, so that many soils have tended to become sandy. In the tropics, however, the silica is washed away preferentially and the iron-rich red silicate soils left behind, called *laterite*, bake hard as brick when dried in the sun, to the despair of those who try to scratch a living from them in India, West Africa, and parts of South America. In the tropical rain-forests, fragile peaty-like soils are built up out of humus from shed leaves, and depend on the trees for protection from the scouring action of torrential rains or the brick-baking heat of the equatorial sun.

9

Living Things

Abundant Life

We live on a planet overflowing with life. From the polar ice to the tropics lies a land covered with plants and scoured by creatures. Of human beings alone, there are now over 3500 million, but this number is easily surpassed by that of eel-worms (nematodes) in a single meadow, or of bacteria in a thimbleful of garden soil. Even the deserts are impregnated with multitudes of seeds waiting, years if necessary, for drops of rain to make them bloom. The surfaces of the oceans swarm with small plankton – drifting plants and creatures. Diatoms, the most abundant of marine plants, sometimes crowd the surface so densely, like floating green meadows, that sea birds get trapped through sheer numbers clogging their feathers. Strange fish and other living things have been pulled out of the depths of the sea, 8 kilometres down; and minute dry spores, floating just as high in the upper air, unfold into tiny organisms when brought down to earth.

Equally remarkable is the variety of living things. The hundreds of thousands of plant species, and millions of animal ones, come in all shapes and sizes – seaweeds, fungi, mosses, ferns, pine trees, beeches, garden flowers, sponges, jellyfish, worms, crocodiles, salmon, dolphins, bees, bats and birds, apes and men – the list could be expanded to fill volumes. And a microscope set on a drop of pond water shows a world of micro-organisms more fantastic than even a Hieronymous Bosch might imagine. The record of the fossils, in the rocks, has disclosed yet another dimension to the variety of species. Today's different types are only a small sample of all the multifarious forms that have existed since life began on earth.

Yet, on further thought, the similarities between living things are even more striking than their differences. What are they all doing, these things? Basically, the same in every case: taking in energy and material from their surroundings and using these to grow themselves and to reproduce their kind. This is the common feature of all life, however various the means of accomplishing it.

The main division, today, is in the ways of obtaining energy. Green *plants* absorb sunlight to photosynthesise their food from simple inorganic chemicals. Their chlorophyll molecules hold water which is then split by high-energy photons into oxygen and hydrogen. The oxygen goes off into the environment and the hydrogen reacts with carbon dioxide to make various *carbohydrates*, such as glucose sugar (6 carbon atoms, 12 hydrogens, 6 oxygens), starch, glycogen, and cellulose, which are aggregates of such molecules. These are stored in the plants as reserves of fuel whose energy is released, as and when required, by processes of oxidation which in effect reverse the photosynthesis. *Animals*, on the other hand, cannot use sunlight directly and get their photosynthetic energy second-hand by eating plants, so taking over their sugar and other substances, or by eating other animals which in turn have built themselves up by the same direct or indirect feeding on plant life; as is said, 'all flesh is grass'.

Growing organisms need materials as well as energy. The productivity of oceans and great lakes is restricted mainly by the scarcity in them of chemical nutrients, so that where agricultural fertilisers get washed off the land into such waters they sometimes encourage algae and bacteria to multiply extravagantly, choking out other life and eliminating dissolved oxygen (eutrophication). The small floating plankton plants, on which all marine life ultimately depends, have to explore large volumes of water, by slowly sinking and then being swept back again by upwellings, to find the thinly spread nutrients. On land, where such movement is not possible, a plant needs widespread roots, in good contact with water and dissolved mineral nutrients between the grains of soil. To get its sunlight and carbon dioxide it also needs a head of leaves, above ground, held up on a stalk from the roots. As water is evaporated from the leaves – a vigorous plant can in this way *transpire* an amount of water equal to half its weight in one day – more water is sucked up channels in the stalk, from the roots, bringing dissolved nitrates, phosphates and other nutrients.

Because it lives by eating, an animal is organised very differently. Essentially it is a *tube*, open at its mouth end for taking in food, and at its anus end for eliminating indigestible waste. The tube itself is basically a gut or intestine, sometimes elaborated also into a stomach and other features, in which the food is partly decomposed and absorbed into the body. Most animals have to forage for food and so have to slither, wriggle or worm their way about or, if they are lucky, use their fins, wings or legs. Their movements need to be guided by sensors such as eyes, ears and noses, the information from which has to be co-ordinated by a brain, at the centre of a communications network of nerves. Being physically active, animals 'burn up' large amounts of food throughout their bodies and so need a major system for breathing, spreading oxygen around their bodies, and collecting and removing waste products. In the higher animals this need is met by the blood, pumped by the heart to the various parts of the body, with lungs or gills for regenerating it with oxygen from the air or water of the environment, and with kidneys and bladder for cleaning it and discharging waste products as urine.

All this elaboration in the organisms of the higher animals comes from their different method of obtaining energy. In the other key function of a living thing, its *reproduction*, there are close similarities between the plant and animal kingdoms. Individual organisms are not immortal and each species perpetuates itself through the production of new generations from old. Most plants and animals reproduce *sexually*, eggs from the female parent being fertilised by sperm from the male. The offspring so produced inherit from both parents so that the species becomes more varied and better able to survive.

The eggs and sperm must meet. Many sea fish such as herring simply pour out millions of eggs from the female, or sperm from the male which swim by wriggling their whiplike flagella, and fertilisation occurs between the few which happen to meet. The rest die. Sometimes, as with salmon, the male accompanies the female and does not discharge sperm until the eggs are laid, which greatly reduces the waste. It is even more efficient to produce few eggs and keep them in the body until fertilised. In any case, on land, where there is no watery environment to sustain tiny eggs and sperm, such a method is more or less essential.

Flowering plants reproduce by fertilisation inside the parent. The eggs are sheltered in the ovary at the centre of the flower and the male sperm carried as grains of pollen on the stamens. Some plants fertilise themselves with their own pollen. With others the pollen spreads from one to another, being blown in the wind or carried as dust on the bodies of visiting insects seeking nectar. The fertilised eggs, supplied with stores of food and tough cases, are released as seeds, to germinate.

Beetles, reptiles and birds also lay eggs in tough protective cases or shells. Again, fertilisation happens beforehand, by mating, the sperm being introduced into the female duct by an external male organ. It is a great advantage to keep the fertilised eggs inside the mother's body during their early development, so that the offspring can be born in an already advanced condition. In the higher mammals, the young are thus nourished in the womb from the mother's blood, through the placenta. While the general method of mating remains the same in all these cases, there are extraordinary variations. Thus, some types of octopus develop a special arm filled with sperm which breaks off and swims away by itself to find a female.

Although the classification of plants and animals into distinct species, first done systematically by Linnaeus, greatly helps organised study, there is a more or less continuous gradation from one kind to another, with no really firm boundaries. There are animals such as sea-anemones and sponges which sit, plantlike, waiting for food to come their way; and plants such as Venus's flytrap which catch and eat insects to supplement their food supplies. There are plants and fungi with no chlorophyll which get their food from decaying organic matter or by living like parasites on the tissues of their hosts. At primitive levels the distinction between plant and animal sometimes disappears completely. The scum on a stagnant pond often consists of a small organism, the *euglena*, which like any other green plant uses sunlight to make food. But in the dark it loses its colour and swims about catching food, as an animal. Another example is *chrysamoeba*, a shapeless, jelly-like, organism living in water. It can live as a green plant. But it can also live like a kind of animal, crawling along surfaces by an oozing motion in which it reshapes its body to make 'feet', which are retracted again as it moves along, and catching organisms by enfolding them in several such 'feet'.

The Art of Survival

The immortality denied to individuals is granted to their species, or nearly so. Fossil ants found in amber 30 million years old are practically the same as those alive today. The oysters of 150 million years ago, if swept forward in Einstein's time machine, could be eaten today in any restaurant. The 'standard production run' for a species of a larger animal is rather shorter than this, but lasts a few million years. It is interesting to relate these long production runs to the number of 'models' produced.

For this, a useful notion is that of the *doubling time of pure exponential growth*, i.e. the number of years it takes for a steadily growing species to double its numbers. The percentage growth of the population in one year is then roughly equal to 70 divided by the doubling time. For example, our own species is doubling in numbers worldwide in about 35 years at present, i.e. growing at about 2 per cent a year.

It now numbers about 3500 million. Divide this number repeatedly by 2, to take us back through the sequence of doubling times, and we find that it needs about 32 such divisions to get back to a single pair, an imaginary primeval Adam and Eve. Our species has certainly been in existence for something like 1 million years, so that 32 doublings implies an average doubling time of about 30,000 years, or a growth rate of about 0.002 per cent a year. In fact, the figures must be even more extreme than this. Before we began to domesticate plants and animals, about 10,000 years ago – a mere tick of the geological clock – our population could not have exceeded 10 millions, which on the same argument implies an average growth rate of only about 0.0015 per cent a year before then.

In other words, through all that time the numbers hardly increased, on average, from one century to the next. It has been just the same with all the other established species of animals and plants, through all the ups and downs of good years and bad, despite their intrinsic fecundity. Evidently, where the population of a given species becomes dense, the average individual has much less chance of surviving and leaving offspring. There are many reasons for this. Malthus, in his famous Essay on Population (1798), argued that while an unchecked population increases in geometric progression – which today we call exponential growth – its provision of food grows only in arithmetic progression, so that a point must come when food supply will limit a population, if nothing else does. For example, shortage of winter food keeps down the numbers of birds and wild animals in northern countries. Again, in northern forests, the dense canopy of trees cuts off sunlight at ground level, so that the seeds dropped there cannot thrive unless existing trees die, or are removed, to make room for them. In tropical forests, on the other hand, if one type of tree becomes abundant those insects that specialise in eating it will multiply rapidly and cut it back again, so that a stable community of many different kinds of tree is developed.

Many species are limited by serving as food for others, or because they depend on others for their food. The living world is a web of *food chains*. Insects eat plants and one another, but are eaten by small birds which themselves may fall prey to certain larger ones. Small shell-fish eat plankton and are then eaten by mackerel, a food for tuna which in turn may be eaten by man. These predators and their prey are, furthermore, also food for parasites and the micro-organisms of disease, and their dead bodies feed the bacteria which decompose them. Each species in a natural chain develops to a best size of population, in relation to the other species, because of the way they all depend on one another, and a stable mixed society of species forms. Only about one-tenth of the food eaten by a growing animal becomes its own flesh, so that most chains run out after a few stages, and the numbers in each stage are ultimately determined by the availability of the plant food on which they all depend.

The Law of Nature

Able to multiply their numbers, but lacking the means, understanding or will to control their birth rate voluntarily, most species are swept remorselessly on to the numbers at which the struggle for existence – or more exactly the competition for the chance to reproduce – limits their populations. The moorland grouse, for example, depends on heather for its food and protection. Cock birds aggressively claim and defend their territories, each patrolling his own patch, large enough to rear and feed one family. The unsuccessful claimants are driven off the moors, in winter, to open areas where they cannot feed and fall victim to predators. But the species as a whole is preserved, in the proper numbers for the moor, and indeed is improved since its strongest members win the struggle.

We have reached the famous 'survival of the fittest' which underlay the thinking of Darwin and Wallace in their discovery of the immense principle which drives the biological world: *evolution by natural selection*. They knew – as we all do simply by looking at people around us – that individuals are different, even within the same species. Some are tall, others short; some can run quickly, others are big-boned and heavily-built; some have sharp eyesight, others hear keenly. Darwin and Wallace realised that, in the struggle for existence, such variations would give some individuals an advantage over others and thus a better chance to produce offspring. They also knew about *heredity*, as demonstrated in the familiar efforts of animal and plant breeders: that parents reproduce their own features in their offspring; and also that breeders can – by systematically selecting breeding pairs in which certain features are prominent – gradually evolve strains, over a number of generations, in which those features are enormously developed.

Darwin and Wallace's great discovery was that selective breeding occurs *naturally*, through the survival of the fittest, and that over the long reaches of time, through the millions of generations, this simple principle acting relentlessly over and over again, has evolved all the variety of modern life – all the higher forms, gifted with marvellous eyes, limbs, brains, etc. – from the primitive organisms of the early earth. The continuous evolution of species was already strongly suspected, in scientific circles, by the mid-19th century. Geologists and palaeontologists, digging through the rocks, had traced continuous changes back from today's creatures to seemingly quite different ancestors, millions of years old; and anatomists had found the structures of organs such as kidneys, in various species, to be so similar, down to fine points of detail, that any explanation other than in terms of a continuous family relationship was quite incredible.

Darwin and Wallace realised that evolution occurs because some members of a population, through individual variations, are better suited than most to leave offspring, in the face of growing competition from all others trying to do the same. We can see it in action today. For example, there is a type of moth, once always white, which has recently become dark in and near cities. This moth rests on tree trunks in the daytime, where it may get eaten by birds. There has been a recent evolution of colour, by natural selection. The dark variety merges inconspicuously into the background on the grime-blackened trunks of city trees.

The struggle for existence, by selectively breeding those individuals best suited to produce offspring in the conditions of their local environment, provides the great engine which has driven life forwards, through the millennia, to today's complex and highly evolved forms. This simple great principle is the general law of nature for the biological world, as all-pervasive for it as is universal gravitation for the physical world. It works so marvellously, in producing all kinds of complex creatures, with intricate and perfectly functioning organs, so well suited to their surroundings, that it is hard to resist thinking that these have been consciously and separately designed. But what causes the individual variations on which the selection acts? For this we have to look at how organisms are made.

Grains of Life

The microscopists of the 17th century first saw tissue, not as a featureless substance, but a mosaic of small boxes called *cells*; and by the 19th century it was known that all plants and animals are made this way. Cells come in various shapes and sizes. Among the biggest are the yolks of eggs, each a single cell, but the typical body cell is about a hundredth of a millimetre across, and bacterial cells are even smaller. There are roughly rectangular or honeycomb-shaped cells in plants, round egg cells, tadpole-like sperm cells, hairy cells, sliver-shaped muscle cells, long cable-like nerve cells, and many other shapes.

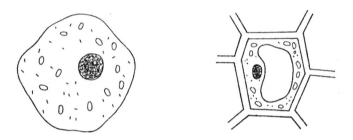

An animal cell, in its soft membrane, and a plant cell, the membrane of which is supported by a stiff cellulose case. The large dark-stained nucleus, in both cells, floats in the cytoplasm, which also contains various other globules. The most prominent of these are the mitochondria, which are the power houses of the cell; and, in plant cells only, the chloroplasts which contain green chlorophyll. The clear central region in the plant cell is the vacuole, which contains plant sap.

The cell is the unit of life, the 'atom' of the living world. Simple organisms such as the amoeba, euglena and bacteria, are themselves just single cells. A large plant or animal, on the other hand, is an organised community of cells – millions of millions of them – each of which is a self-contained unit organism that looks after itself, absorbing nutrients from its local environment much like a free single-cell organism, yet contributing to the corporate activity of its community. If cells from living animal tissue are placed in a suitable 'soup' of nutrients, in the technique of *tissue culture*, they can go on living on their own, as independent single-celled creatures.

A cell is a blob of jelly-like fluid, the *protoplasm* or *cytoplasm*, held in a thin 'plastic bag' *membrane*, through the wall of which the cell absorbs suitable food molecules from its surroundings. A plant cell also has a stiff cellulose outer case for support. Suspended in the fluid are various kinds of small globules, including in plant cells those green ones that contain the chlorophyll for photosynthesis. The most striking globule in a cell is the *nucleus*, which holds the *chromosomes* – the very heart of life – given this name because they are easily stained by dyes used to make them visible in the microscope. They are best seen just before a cell is about to reproduce, when they look like little rods or threads of various lengths, some bent, spread about the nucleus. In the higher plants and animals, which reproduce sexually, each body cell contains *two* of each kind of chromosome, and cells in which the chromosomes come in such pairs are known as *diploid*. In man there are 23 pairs of different chromosomes in each diploid cell. This is not a particularly distinguished number; the potato has 24.

By absorbing molecules of food through its membrane, combining some of them with oxygen to make energy and turning others into its own body substance, a cell thrives and grows. When it reaches a certain size it usually divides into two 'daughter' cells, just like itself, in the process known as *mitosis*. In a single-celled organism, there are then two living things in place of one. In multi-celled organisms, the daughter cells usually stay together, so adding to their piece of tissue. In man, and higher plants and animals, all this begins with the fertilised egg, the single cell from which the complete being grows by repeated mitosis. The egg first divides into two, these in turn divide into four, then eight, and so on, through fifty or sixty generations to the whole man. As they multiply, various cells become specialised for particular purposes and organs – noses, fingers, brains, kidneys – and their rates of multiplication adjust themselves to produce a well-turned-out individual. During vigorous growth the rates are very high; thus a baby, growing an ounce a day, makes thousands more cells every second.

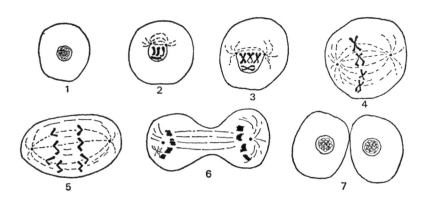

Multiplication of a body cell by mitosis. At first the chromosomes are dispersed throughout the nucleus. Then (2) they condense into short thick rods and part of the nuclear cell wall opens up to two 'spindles'. The thick rods become clearly twinned (3 and 4) and the spindles move apart. The two members of each chromosome twin are then pulled by the spindles to opposite sides of the cell (5), where they begin to disperse locally, and the cell finally divides to make two cells (6 and 7).

The chromosomes are at the centre of all this. As a cell grows, each of its original set of chromosomes becomes thicker and eventually splits along its length into two strands, both complete chromosomes, perfect reproductions of itself. All the original chromosomes thicken and split at the same time so that there is a brief stage when the cell contains *twice* its ordinary number of chromosomes, i.e. it then has *four* samples of each of its basic kinds, two strands from each member of each pair. This is an unstable situation however, and the chromosomes are drawn apart into two equal groups, each containing one of the two strands from every split. Each group is thus a complete set, a reproduction of the original set before it began to thicken. These two groups then rearrange themselves, in opposite sides of the cell, into two nuclei, and a membrane wall forms across the cell, dividing them. And so two daughter cells are created, each enclosed in a complete membrane and possessing its own nucleus, just like that of the original cell. These daughter cells in turn also grow, their chromosomes thicken and split, and the cycle is repeated.

Whereas a multi-celled organism *grows* by just this division of its cells, it cannot of course *reproduce* itself by simply dividing into two. In sexual reproduction the fertilised offspring cell is produced by the union of an egg cell with a sperm cell, from its parents. If these were ordinary cells, it would then have twice as many chromosomes as its parents, one complete set of pairs from each. Its own offspring would have twice as many again, and so on. This nonsense is avoided through the fact that the reproductive or *gamete* cells in the parents have only *half* the normal number of chromosomes. We have seen that a normal body cell (diploid) has a standard number of *pairs* of chromosomes, 23 of them in man, and that when it divides there is a stage where it has twice as many as this, i.e. *four* complete sets of single chromosomes. This happens also in the creation of the gamete cells, in the uterus or testes, but instead of a division into two there is now one into *four* cells, each containing only *one* set of chromosomes, not two paired sets. These are the special *haploid* cells, formed by this fourfold division known as *meiosis*, which are used in sexual reproduction. In the male they become four sperm cells, and in the female one of them grows into a large egg cell while the others generally remain small. When an egg cell is fertilised, by taking in a sperm cell, it then possesses a pair of sets of chromosomes, one from each parent. Now a diploid cell, it is ready to embark on life's course and multiply

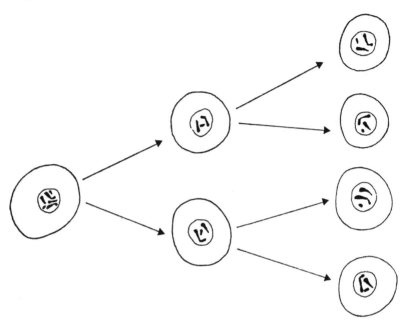

Formation of four haploid cells by meiosis. The first step produces two cells containing half the original number of chromosomes and, in the second step, each of these two cells exactly
duplicates itself.

into a new being. In this way a sexually reproduced offspring
carries, in its two sets of chromosomes, some characteristics
from each parent, which increases the diversity of the species.

Family Trees

Children of course generally look like their parents. A
daughter may have 'her father's eyes, her mother's nose'.
But it is not all that simple. Everyone in the family is different (unless there happen to be identical twins) and new
features may appear. For example, brown-eyed parents may
have a blue-eyed child.

　　Mendel, in the mid-19th century, discovered how nature
arranges all this. He bred garden peas. By choosing a certain

character of the plant for study – for example, tallness or shortness – he developed and selected *pure-bred* tall plants, i.e. those which when mated with their own kind always produced tall offspring, and he similarly produced pure-bred short plants. Next, he mated pure-bred tall with pure-bred short ones, to produce *cross-bred* offspring. All these were tall, which he explained on the assumption that, in the mixed and contradictory characteristics implanted in the cross-bred offspring, the one for tallness *dominated* the one for shortness, which was suppressed. This is found quite generally for all contradictory pairs of characteristics, which are described as *dominant* and *recessive*, respectively.

Mendel then mated the tall cross-bred plants with one another and showed that these produced both tall and short offspring, on average three tall for each short one. From discoveries such as this, and through a magnificent piece of analysis, he deduced that each character is carried from parents to offspring by *two* units now called *genes*. Our most basic inheritance is a set of genes. They direct the cells in their development and functioning, and determine what is to grow from the fertilised egg, whether it is to be an oak tree or a man, have fins or legs, dark or light hair.

In an ordinary body cell there are two genes – one of which may be dominant, the other recessive – for each characteristic. Mendel also deduced that in the formation of the sex cells these two genes separate, one going to each. He had in fact inferred, from the patterns of heredity shown by his plants, precisely that behaviour in the genes that the microscopists were later to discover in the chromosomes. We shall look below at the obvious connection between them. An egg cell, then, has a single set of genes, as also does a sperm cell. When they mate, the fertilised egg possesses two sets, one from each parent. In pure-bred strains, both genes of a pair determine the same characteristic, but in cross-bred strains they may act in contradiction, in which case one will dominate and decide what the offspring is to be like.

From this marvellously simple but elegant system flow all the richly diverse patterns of heredity. Consider for example the colours of our eyes. The gene responsible may be the dominant 'B' for brown eyes or the recessive 'b' for blue ones. A blue-eyed parent must then be a 'bb', i.e. both genes must be of the 'b' type; but a brown-eyed one may be either 'BB' or 'Bb', since in this latter case the gene for brown will dominate over that for blue. There are various possibilities for their offspring. The 'BB' parent must have brown-eyed children, but the equally brown-eyed 'Bb' has a half chance of blue-eyed children if mated with a 'bb', since the recessive 'b' gene may be passed on instead of the dominant 'B'. Indeed, two brown-eyed 'Bb' parents have a quarter chance of producing a blue-eyed child, since 'bb' is among the four possible combinations of one gene from each.

Chromosomes behave just like Mendel's genes but a cell contains a few only, whereas multitudes of genes are needed to determine all the characters of a large organism. Under a powerful microscope, however, a chromosome looks like a necklace of a thousand or two small platelike 'beads', which appear as dark bands running across the line of the thread. The suspicion that these might be genes was confirmed by Morgan's discovery that a sudden genetic change in an evolving family of fruit flies – the formation of stubby wings, for example – was accompanied by a corresponding change in the band structure of a chromosome. In recent years it has become possible to map out along chromosomes the places – the genes in fact – responsible for various particular features of organisms.

When a cell divides, the genes carried on different chromosomes may go into different cells, whereas those on the same chromosome of course stay together (except occasionally when two separating chromosomes, entangled in each other, break and their fragments rejoin, cross-wise). All those characteristics carried on a single chromosome are thus inherited together and are said to be *linked*. Examples of this are provided by those characters which happen to be carried on the chromosomes which determine the sex of an organism. There are two different sex chromosomes, denoted by X and Y, and the X one carries many more other characters than the Y. The pair of sex chromosomes is XX in a female and XY in a male, so that the fertilized egg gets one X from its mother and either an X or Y from its father. It thus has an equal chance of becoming female (XX) or male (XY).

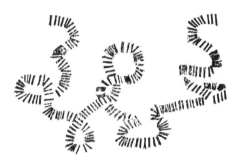

A piece of chromosome, showing the banded gene structure.

An interesting example of linked characteristics occurs when a recessive gene is carried on an X but is not matched by any corresponding character on the Y. Consider, for example, colour blindness. A woman carrying the gene for this on only one of her X chromosomes is not colour blind, because the 'normal' gene on her other X is dominant, but if her son inherits this recessive gene he is colour blind because he has nothing to counteract it on his father's Y. A more serious example is haemophilia, in which the blood fails to clot. The most famous case was Queen Victoria who carried the recessive gene for this on one of her X chromosomes. King Edward VII inherited her other X so that the haemophilic gene passed out of the British royal family. But some of her daughters inherited it and their daughters in turn, one of whom married the last Tsar. The story of their haemophilic son, during the days leading up to the Russian revolution, is now part of history.

Genes normally copy themselves with wonderful accuracy,

through the generations, but occasionally something goes wrong and one of them is changed unpredictably into an arbitrarily different gene. This new gene, from such a *mutation*, may then also copy itself, like any other, and pass into the succeeding generations, producing a sudden new strain, a 'quantum' of change in some feature of a population: stubby wings on a fly; a white rabbit or dark moth; a susceptibility to haemophilia; or, as in the great influenza outbreak of 1918–19, a virulent killer from a previously mild strain. The stability of genes and the sudden all-or-nothing nature of their mutations suggest that genes are molecules which normally maintain their structures intact but which also occasionally suffer rearrangements. In fact, high-energy photons from X-rays and other radiations as well as certain chemical compounds (*mutagens*) promote mutations, as is to be expected if a mutation is a disturbance and resettling in different positions of the atoms in a genetic molecule.

Because established populations are usually well adapted to their conditions of life the changes produced by most mutations are generally harmful. Fortunately the mutant gene is often recessive relative to the normal one so that in sexual reproduction the change remains usually suppressed, except where there is close inbreeding which increases the chance of an offspring receiving the same mutant from both parents. But mutant genes are not always recessive. A big mutant change is usually very harmful. It may be lethal to its possessor or its offspring; or it may produce barrenness. Mostly, small mutant changes are also bad. But not always. Occasionally there is a favourable change, one that happens to give its inheritors an advantage over their fellows, enabling them to multiply more and so, along with their mutant gene, gradually become the normal type for their population.

This is the great, simple, secret of evolution, that random mutation produces the variations on which natural selection acts. The giraffe did not get its neck by stretching but was simply given it by chance. Those of its fellows that were not so accidentally favoured gradually lost their position in the struggle for survival. All the richly endowed varieties of modern life – the forest oak, the tiger burning bright, the noble piece of work that is man – have evolved by blind chance aided and abetted by the slow, inexorable, grind of natural selection.

IO

The Chemistry of Creation

Molecules at Work

Let us now, in imagination, look into a cell so intimately that we see its atoms, what they are, how arranged and what doing. This is not really possible, but the discoveries of the chemists and molecular biologists have nevertheless now unravelled the molecular basis of life. The atoms we find are of course quite familiar: mainly carbon, hydrogen, oxygen, and nitrogen, with small amounts of phosphorus and traces of many others.

The interest is in how they are arranged in molecules and what they are doing. The most common substance is water – three-quarters of our own bodies – for the protoplasm is a jelly of various molecules and globules in water. As well as oxygen and nutrients such as glucose and ammonia, pumped into the cell through its membrane from outside, there are many molecules made by the cell itself. Most are fairly small, hardly more than a dozen atoms or so, but some are giant molecules with tens of thousands of atoms strung together into a long-chain polymer. There are few middle-sized polymers, which is perhaps not surprising since a repetitive process is needed to join numbers of similar small molecules together, end to end, and the thing about repetition is that it simply goes on and on.

There are four main kinds of organic molecules in the cell: *carbohydrates* such as glucose, other sugars and glycogen: *fats*, i.e. hydrocarbon strings and glycogen linked through a fatty acid *carboxyl* group (carbon, oxygen, oxygen, hydrogen) as mentioned in chapter 8; *proteins*; and *nucleic acids*. The first three of these are familiar in our foods, from the tissues of plants and animals, and we absorb them into our own cells. The fourth – nucleic acids – are less abundant but their function is quite literally the vital one, transforming blind chemistry into creative life.

There are many different kinds of proteins, which are the work-horse molecules of life. They are found in membranes, tendon and skin, and as *collagen* in bone or *keratin* in hair, where their jobs are structural; as also in muscle, in which the *myosin* protein fibres show a remarkable ability to contract and relax back again. Many proteins have important chemical roles, such as the red *haemoglobin* molecule which carries oxygen in the blood from the lungs to the tissues; and its close relative, the *myoglobin* molecule which takes over this oxygen and stores it until needed by the cell. Again, there is the protein *lysosome*, in teardrops, which destroys bacteria; *insulin*, which enables the body to use glucose; and various other *hormone* proteins which travel through the blood and modulate bodily functions.

But perhaps the most fascinating proteins are the *enzymes*, the organic catalyst molecules which enable various chemical reactions in the cell to occur, without themselves being consumed in these reactions. Their name comes from the Greek for 'in yeast', because these proteins, in yeast cells, ferment sugar into alcohol as a – for them – by-product of their extracting energy from sugar in the absence of oxygen (which is the essence of *fermentation*) for the benefit of their cells. In a yeast cell a molecule of sugar is taken through a sequence of twelve different chemical reactions, each fairly simple in itself, to turn it into alcohol. It is rather like turning a long word such as, for example, *rhododendron*, into say *dodecahedron*, in steps, by adding or subtracting in each step the letters required for a short word. Each step is made possible by the presence of an enzyme, special for that step, which works on that particular process in the 'production line' and no other.

A cell has thousands of different kinds of enzymes, each looking after its own particular reaction. They are the 'machine tools' of the cell and are remarkable in both their specificity and their speed of action. A cell is a turmoil of furious activity; molecules and particles are constantly being ingested, transformed, and ejected. A bacterial cell for example can make a complete copy of itself in about twenty minutes. A cell's individual reactions can often be repeated in the laboratory, but not their speed, which it owes to the immense chemical virtuosity of its enzymes, each molecule of which may get through something like a hundred jobs a second.

A cell is thus a prodigious chemical factory, enormous in output for its size, but also extremely subtle. It is not a mass-production plant, churning out heaps of simple molecules by blind chemistry – even though its enzymes transform many times their own amount of material – but a made-to-measure shop, producing complicated molecules according to individual specification and particular demand. It is also very adaptable, varying the activity of its enzymes to suit changes in its environment, so as to continue making more of itself as regularly and efficiently as possible.

Cells of course need *energy*, both for these manufactures and for their external functions, from the swimming of sperm and euglena cells to the root spreading and transpiration of plants and the flexing of muscles in animals. Much of the cell's machinery is concerned with fuel and power supplies. Many chemical reactions are necessary to make sugar from water, carbon dioxide and photons; to clump the sugar molecules into starch and other large carbohydrates; and to build up fats for long-term energy storage, particularly in animals; as well as to release the energy in the cells as and when required.

These *metabolic* reactions are governed by various enzymes, which are mainly sited in small globules known as *mito-*

chondria, dispersed through the cytoplasm, which are the power-houses of the cell. In plants the chlorophyll-bearing globules, which absorb carbon dioxide and release oxygen, stop working at night; but the mitochondria keep going, running the reverse reactions which release the stored energy for their plant. This is why cut flowers freshen the air in a room during daylight hours, but are best removed from bedrooms at night.

It is a great over-simplification to think of the energy-releasing processes as photosynthesis in reverse, especially since the energy needs to be built into various chemical substances, not released as a flash of light. The first step in both plants and animals is to break down the large energy-storage molecules into glucose. Then, again in both plants and animals, there are two possibilities for 'burning' this sugar. Given plenty of oxygen it can go all the way to the final products, water and carbon dioxide. But if oxygen is scarce it can stop at the intermediate stage of *fermentation*, yielding products – such as alcohol in yeast and lactic acid in muscle – which are still rich in energy that could be released by further oxidation.

The glucose molecules are taken apart in several stages, serviced by about twenty enzymes, and much of their energy is stored in molecules of 'ATP' that are put together in these reactions. ATP is a compound of a certain organic substance, A (for adenosine), with tri-phosphate, i.e. three phosphate molecules (each a phosphorus atom with oxygen attachments) which are linked together in bonds which store their energy. It is the source of ready energy for running the molecular machinery, in all cells, and it works by taking part in the various chemical reactions going on in the cell, breaking down into smaller phosphate groups and so stimulating the reacting molecules, with energy, into configurations suitable for the next stage of molecular construction.

Chemical Virtuosity

The thousands of different proteins in a cell belong to a single great family, the same in all living things. The secret of their enormous diversity is as simple as our using an alphabet of only 26 letters to write all manner of long sentences. The individual 'letters' in proteins are *amino-acid* molecules. There is a basic alphabet of just 20 of these, together with a few variants. These letters are strung together in hundreds, to form a long-chain polymer, in a sequence which seems to be random but is in fact absolutely precise and crucial, for it governs the performance of its particular protein molecule. These sequences are vital to the proper working of the cell and very few mistakes can be tolerated.

Each amino-acid has a central carbon atom with four chemical bonds. What happens to three of these is characteristic of the family. One goes to a hydrogen atom; another to an *amine* group – one nitrogen and two hydrogen atoms – related to ammonia; and the third to a carboxyl group. These common parts of amino-acid molecules can link up to form polymer chains. Each such link is made by removing one water molecule from two amino-acid molecules. This is done by taking a hydrogen atom off the amine end of one, and a hydroxyl off the carboxyl end of the other to make the water molecule; and the two 'stumps' are then joined to unite the amino-acid molecules at their points of amputation. Each of these amino-acids still has its other end available for similar treatment, to link up with other amino-acid molecules, and so form a long chain, the *polypeptide backbone* of the protein.

Now for the fourth bond on each central carbon atom. This sticks out sideways from the chain and has a 'side-group' molecule fixed to it, the simplest of which is a single hydrogen atom. In many other amino-acids it is one of the familiar, small, organic groups – hydrocarbon, hydroxyl, benzene ring, etc. – but it sometimes also contains a sulphur or nitrogen atom in the group. These side-groups sit like 'charms' on the sides of beads in a necklace.

How do proteins work? This depends on the shapes of their molecules. Those such as the *keratin* of hair are fibres. Pauling showed that in these the chain is wound into the so-called *alpha-helix* structure, like a telephone cord, its close turns held together by hydrogen bonds (see chapter 8). But what about enzymes? Here, to go with the apparently random amino-acid sequence, we find an apparently random shape, a crumpling of the chain into a tight round ball, a dense clump of atoms. But we should not mistake complexity for randomness; these *globular proteins* are incredible little machines, precisely shaped to do specific things to specific molecules, and to order.

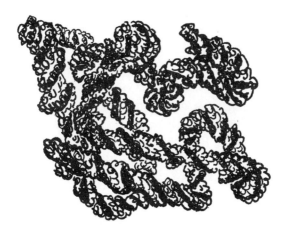

A globular protein.

The first point is that some amino-acids have 'oily' side-groups, such as hydrocarbons, repellent to water, whereas others have slightly 'ionic' ones such as hydroxyl, attractive to water. The open molecular chain, in water, is thus compelled by its side-groups to fold up systematically into a ball with its 'oily' groups buried inside and its 'ionic' ones facing outwards. The ensuing structure is complex, but with each amino-acid precisely chosen and precisely placed. This folding, in and out, produces a knobbly surface with 'caves' in it. One of these is the *active site* where the enzyme does its work. This cave has just the right atomic shape and structure to accept its own particular work-piece molecule; and to hold it, in the cage of surrounding amino-acid active ends, for about long enough to give this captive molecule a chance to accept or release the constituents of a simple molecule, such as water or ammonia, and so undergo its particular increment of chemical change at that site.

There would of course be chaos if all the enzymes simply poured out their products regardless. Their efforts have to be co-ordinated. This is done very sensitively by enzymes which react to their surroundings; so that if, for example, the cell finds itself in an environment rich in amino-acids it will arrange to pump these in through its membrane, from outside, and temporarily shut down its own machinery for making amino-acids. Fine control is arranged through other special sites on the surface of the enzyme, usually away from the active site. Such sites can accept molecules, which are involved in the chemical process in question, and hold them for short periods. These molecules, by the way they impress themselves on the special sites, distort the whole enzyme slightly and change the shape of the active site, enhancing or reducing its effectiveness as the case may be. The production of a given molecule is in this way controlled by the abundances of the various related molecules in the environment.

The marvel is in the complex pattern, which enables proteins to do such intricate and specialised work, so sensitively, by what are basically ordinary 'textbook' properties of matter. Consider, for example, another chemically-active protein, *haemoglobin*. To do its job it has to have two opposite attitudes to oxygen: *taking all*, in the lungs; *giving all*, in the tissues. Its chemical virtuosity is centred on its special *haem* group, a small unit built round an iron atom. The whole haemoglobin molecule is quartered into four sub-molecules, each with its own haem group embedded in its outer surface. When an oxygen molecule attaches itself to a haem group, the iron atom shrinks a little, because electrons are transferred, and it then fits more easily within the group. As a result, the group rearranges itself a little and this slightly distorts the whole molecule, making it *easier* for the other haem groups to take up oxygen, so giving the haemoglobin its vital 'all-or-nothing' attitude to oxygen. This switch from low-affinity to high-affinity occurs by the breaking of some weak bonds between the sub-molecules, strained by the slightly misfitting iron atom in its haem group.

The Language of the Genes

The quest for the 'secret of life' takes us beyond the proteins and on to the nucleic acids. Over 100 years ago Mieschner extracted something which he called nuclein from cell nuclei; and shortly afterwards Hertwig concluded that 'nuclein is the substance responsible not only for fertilisation but also for the transmission of heredity characteristics.' But this was not generally accepted until the 1940s and it was only after the chemical studies of Todd and others that nuclein became characterised as 'DNA', the molecule *deoxyribonucleic acid*.

DNA, like protein, is a polymer with side-groups on the units of the chain. It is extremely long. The total in the 46 chromosomes of a human cell contains over 1000 million units and is about two metres long, all tucked into something about a thousandth of a centimetre across. It is made up of large numbers of three small types of molecules: phosphate, sugar and *nucleotide*. The sugar is *deoxyribose*, a molecule with a five-sided ring. The phosphate and sugar molecules alternate as 'beads' along the chain and each sugar bead has a nucleotide side-group attached to it.

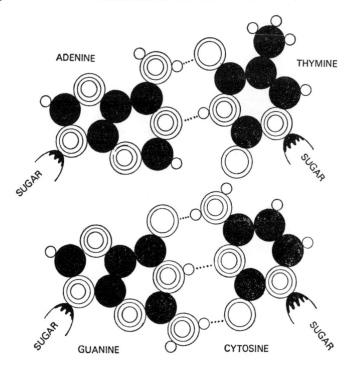

Hydrogen bonds (dotted) between A – T and G – C bases in DNA. The small circles are hydrogen atoms, the double circles are oxygen, the triple ones are nitrogen, and the black ones are carbon. The positions of the carbon atom ends of the sugar molecules, to which the bases are attached, are also shown.

There are four different types of nucleotides, often called *bases*, known as A, G, C, and T, which stand for *adenine, guanine, cytosine* and *thymine*. These are organic molecules containing nitrogen, in the shape of flat rings. A and G are large, consisting of two rings like a figure 8; and C and T are small, having only one ring each. The sequence of these four bases along a thread of DNA appears to be quite random but in fact, like the sequences in protein, it is full of precise meaning. Each gene is a section along the thread. Written in the language of the genes, the sequence is the set of instructions for making a living thing. All the information for what proteins are to be made, listed down to the last amino-acid; for what organs and tissues are to be developed; for whether a fertilised egg is to become a man or minnow— all this is written in the sequence of bases. The information carried on the DNA in a human set of chromosomes, if transcribed into our 26-letter alphabet and set up in print, would fill about 1000 books like this one, all different. This is how much we are worth, in terms of information.

DNA not only carries the genetic information. It passes it on faithfully from cell to cell, through the splitting of the chromosomes. To do this, it must be able to make perfect copies of itself. Crick and Watson puzzled over this in 1953. They knew its chemical composition; they had its X-ray diffraction pattern from the work of Wilkins and Franklin; and they knew of Chargaff's observation that a piece of DNA has the same number of A and T bases, and also the same number of G and C, generally different from the A and T number. Putting these clues together they deduced the famous *double helix* structure. The genetic material consists of *two* DNA chains, side by side, twisted into a spiral.

Picture it as a ladder, the two sugar-phosphate chains making the uprights, twisted round to form a spiral staircase. Each of the flat steps, which connect the uprights regularly, up the ladder, is made of three molecular rings; two belong to a large nucleotide base from one upright, the third belongs to a small base opposite it from the other upright. Where they meet, these bases are linked by hydrogen bonds. A joins to T, in such a step, because they both have two such bonds, and G joins to C because they both have three. This explains Chargaff's rules but, remarkably, all steps formed by these particular base pairs are of the same size and shape and so can be fitted into the same ladder without distortion.

This is a beautiful structure for breeding. Each chain is determined exactly by the other – its *complement* – since for any given base on one there can only be a particular one,

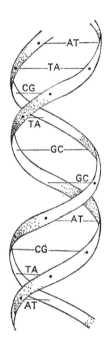

The double helix of DNA. The two spiral uprights, which are long chains of sugar and phosphate molecules, are joined by paired nucleotide bases.

A next to T or G next to C, alongside it on the other. Furthermore, since there are *two* such interlinked chains, which can be separated by breaking the weak hydrogen bonds, faithful duplication can be achieved, for along each single separated chain an exact replica of its original partner can be made. The copying probably begins at one end of the double helix, which unwinds a little to let in sugar, phosphate and nucleotide molecules, together with an enzyme to help assemble them into new chains, each of which then forms a double helix with its template thread. The process works its way along until eventually two complete DNA spirals exist where there was one before. Only rarely is a mistake – a *mutation* – made, such as a single wrong step in the ladder.

This then is the secret of life, the method of multiplying genetic information and transmitting it from cell to cell. But how is the information used? In fact the nuclear DNA does not join in the hurly-burly of the ordinary cell processes.

It is too precious. Instead, it makes a variant of itself, *ribonucleic acid* (RNA), which goes out to direct the making of proteins. In RNA the ribose sugar is slightly different and the T base of DNA is replaced by a U base (for the nucleotide *uracil*, which is similar to thymine). This U pairs with A exactly as T does in DNA. The various items of RNA gather along a strand of DNA in the nucleus which, as in the Watson-Crick process, then lines them up into strands of RNA with the specific pattern set by the DNA. These *messenger-RNA* molecules then go out into the cell to small particles known as *ribosomes* – the 'assembly lines' for making proteins – where the RNA act as 'computer tapes' directing the process. Other shorter pieces of so-called *transfer-RNA* collect amino-acids from the cell and present them to the ribosomes for inclusion in the protein chain in the order set by the messenger-RNA strand.

These are very complex processes but the most interesting question is how the message of the genes, written in the 4-letter alphabet, A, G, C, U, of RNA, is translated into the 20-letter alphabet of the amino-acids in the protein sequences. Nature in fact reads the RNA message as a line of 'three-letter words', the same in all living things. For example, a line beginning as AGCUUCCGU ... is read as AGC, then UUC, CGU ... and so on, each such triplet calling for a particular amino-acid, or serving as a punctuation mark to start or end the message. It has been a great tour de force to decipher this genetic code. The 64 different triplet words are of course more than sufficient for the protein alphabet and in fact two or more often serve the same purpose. For example, glycine, the simplest amino-acid, answers to any of the family GGA, GGU, GGG and GGC, whereas methionine, a more complicated one, answers only to AUG.

Besides the main roles sketched above, nucleic acids have some others. For example, certain lengths of DNA, repeated surprisingly many times over in the chromosomes, appear to be concerned with the processes of moving the chromosomes during cell division, or in controlling the activities of the genes in differently developing cells. RNA is a versatile substance. Even DNA can be made from it, with the help of certain enzymes. And sometimes the sequence of bases along an RNA thread complements itself exactly, in opposite directions, which allows the thread to fold back on itself to join up as a two-stranded stem, with a loop at the end; in this way two- and three-dimensional structures can be made which can give RNA a functional as well as an instructional role.

The pursuit of the main roles is seen at its most ruthless in the *viruses*, organisms built solely for reproduction, in which every function inessential to this key task is stripped right away. They cannot eat, cannot grow, and they reproduce only inside the cells of some other *host* organism, where they are *parasites*, using its chemical machinery and materials to breed themselves. They are extremely small, often much smaller than bacteria, and require the electron microscope for their study. They are the cause of many infective diseases, such as influenza, the common cold, poliomyelitis, smallpox, and some cancers, although not of course the bacterial infections such as typhoid and pneumonia.

There is, for example, the *bacteriophage* virus, which attacks bacteria and provides a fascinating insight into their action generally. It has a *head*, a rigid box of a regular geometric shape reminiscent of the head of a machine bolt, inside which its nucleic acid is crumpled up like a ball of string. Sticking out from the head is a tube surrounded by a spiral spring. It looks like – and indeed acts as – a hypodermic syringe. Fanning out regularly from a base plate at the end of the spring is a spray of thin fibres. The phage attaches itself by the ends of these fibres to a bacterial cell and releases its spring which, contracting, pushes the end of the tube into the cell and discharges its nucleic acid into it. Inside the cell the nucleic acid 'takes over' the machinery, like a crew of pirates, and by its orders forces the cell to make and assemble the parts for new virus particles. After a few minutes the job is done and a hundred or more virus particles burst out of the now ruined cell to seek new pastures.

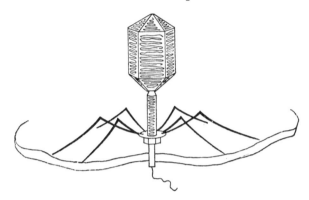

A phage virus about to inject its thread of nucleic acid into a bacterial cell, down the syringe it has pushed through the cell's membrane.

This is typical. A virus is a very simple organism, little more than a strand, usually of RNA although sometimes of DNA, with a box to protect it. The strand is generally only a few thousand bases long, which cannot carry a great message, just enough for the structural protein of its box and its few enzymes. The elaborate machinery for making proteins is absent; the host provides that, as well as the energy for it. The brevity of the message also explains the geometrical simplicity of viruses, so that they often look more like man-made gadgets than natural organisms. With not much information available, something austere is essential, such as prefabricated triangles of proteins which can be joined up edge to edge to make a regular box from their facets.

What is Life?

Viruses demonstrate the versatility and inexorable logic of natural selection. In a world of easy living it is an advantage to have only a short length of nucleic acid, since this can obviously be made and multiplied faster. Once evolution had reached the stage of making cells rich in the basic constituents of life, including even the 'machine tools' for assembling them into proteins when instructed by an RNA 'computer tape', it became possible for these parasites to evolve.

But are they 'alive'? Whereas the simplest cells are self-contained, and will grow and multiply on non-living nutrients, viruses are not. Pure viruses can be crystallised and kept inertly, like other chemicals. They are little more than computer tapes stored in boxes. Only inside a living cell do these tapes find their way to the machine tools and set them to work making copies. Yet they are perhaps a late feature of evolution, versions of RNA and DNA which became 'viable' only after DNA had evolved far enough to make cells.

But what is life, anyway? Is it a bare molecule of nucleic acid, replicating itself in a test-tube, as is now known to be possible? Or is it the whole panoply of the higher organisms, developed from chance mutations by natural selection as increasingly complex means of ensuring the perpetuation of various lines of nucleic acid? In fact it seems to be almost impossible to give a logically satisfactory definition of life. Is 'ability to reproduce' the criterion? But this would include simple crystals in saturated solutions and rule out, for example, mules and worker bees. Is it the ability to synthesise complex molecules from simple ones? This would rule out viruses but include almost any solid surface such as clay that can loosely hold and introduce molecules to one another. Is it the ability to organise information; in the words of chapter 4, to filter out the valuable ordered component [of energy] and turn it into some even more highly organised and complex things? But this would include heat pumps, refrigerators, and automatic factories.

The difficulties of definition spring from the immense variety, continuity and complexity of the biological world.

Because of the variety, there are usually exceptions to defeat any generalisation. The continuity between species, particularly when one goes backwards in time to the branch-points from which different species evolved, and further back still to the first organic molecules, means that no sharp dividing line exists at which one can justifiably say 'on this side *life*, on that side not'.

The complexity raises a difficulty of a different kind. Looking at a tiger, a flowering cherry tree, or even at a bacteriophage, it seems incredible that such a complex organism, with its beautiful harmony between structure and function, owes itself to nothing more than physics and chemistry. Surely it contains some 'vitalism', some special spark, beyond the scope of the physical world, that breathes life into it? But our objective answer has to be that, if there is such a vital spark it does not show itself, nor is it necessary. The reason is that, while there are still many blank spots in this part of our understanding, we can now see how the molecular processes of the physical world are sufficient in themselves to make complex things containing all the features we find in things undoubtedly alive. The matching of chemicals on template molecules, catalysis, polymerisation, the mutation of molecules, are all features of the physical world. Even natural selection has its inorganic counterparts, for example in the competitive growths of crystals in a weak solution. Most large natural crystals contain dislocations because, when an embryonic crystal suffers a physical 'mutation' that dislocates it, the perpetual growth ledges which are then formed on its faces give it the advantage of being able to grow faster than its undislocated companions.

We can, then, take things which are certainly alive and find nothing in their structures or functions that contradicts physics and chemistry or seems beyond the ability of physico-chemical processes. Everything that living things do can be done by atoms performing strictly according to the laws of mechanics, electrodynamics, thermodynamics, and quantum chemistry. But these laws have enabled some combinations of atoms to come together in patterns of extreme complexity in which certain standard physical and chemical behaviours are enhanced and modulated to an almost miraculous degree, thereby enabling these organisms to preserve and reproduce themselves by reacting to their environment with exquisite subtlety and to develop still more sensitive responses.

II

From Molecules to Men

The First Step

A ball of barren rock, in four thousand million years, has
become a world of teeming life. How did it happen? We
know from Pasteur that 'life comes only from life' and from
Darwin that today's advanced life came from humble beginnings. The fossil record takes us back through seemingly
endless cycles of 'chickens and eggs' to about 600 million
years ago, to the far edge of the 'Cambrian' period, before
which creatures had no hard shells or backbones to make
their mark on history. But traces of micro-organisms take
us much farther back, to over 3000 million years ago, when
single-celled organisms rather like today's bacteria or blue-
green algae were laid down in what have since become some
African rocks.

The first cells must have formed earlier still, perhaps
3500 million years ago. The remaining 500 million years or
so, back from there to the beginnings of a geologically stable
planet, are a matter for surmise but must contain a first
answer to our question. At the start of that period there was
only bare hot rock, enveloped in clouds of vented gases. At
the end there were waters on the earth, with self-reliant
cells living and multiplying in them. In the years between,
amino-acids and nucleotides must have been produced and
polymerised; a genetic system developed, able to reproduce
nucleic acid in a 4-letter language and to control the 20-
letter language of the proteins; enzymes had to evolve, as

well as metabolic apparatus for handling energy and raw materials; and the whole lot gathered together in semi-porous bags. Few things in later life could be more marvellous than the steps leading to the first cells.

It is now clear that the very first step of all was quite easy. Oparin in 1923 pointed out that the primitive earth's atmosphere was probably 'reducing' – i.e. contained an excess of hydrogen over oxygen – as is indicated by the low state of oxidation in old iron stone rocks. Without ozone to shield this early atmosphere from the sun's chemically disruptive ultra-violet rays and with other sources of molecular violence generally active – lightning strokes, nuclear radiations and volcanic eruptions – there was every opportunity for this reducing mixture of hydrogen, oxygen, carbon and nitrogen, to turn into methane, water vapour, ammonia, and carbon monoxide gases. But Oparin and also Haldane argued that the effects of radiation would not stop at this. These small inorganic molecules, when stripped of one or two electrons or even atoms, or when quivering with excess energy received from radiation or heat, would often combine chemically with one another, so synthesising various 'organic' substances.

In 1953 Miller, working with Urey, made a great experiment which examined this in the most direct way. Inside a clean chemical flask he created an imitation of the early earth, as imagined by Oparin and Haldane. Hot water in the bottom represented the early oceans. Above it was a mixture of methane, ammonia, hydrogen and water vapour, through which electric sparks were passed for several days. Many biologically important molecules were found to have been synthesised in the flask, including several amino-acids, ribose sugar, and constituents of ATP. Repetitions of the experiment have confirmed these results, with many kinds of reducing atmosphere, and all the component molecules of the genetic system have now been made by these non-biological processes, under conditions similar to those which are believed to have existed on the early earth.

It is probable that very large amounts of these substances were produced in the earth's atmosphere, over the long stretches of primeval time. If lightning was as common then as now, and only 1 per cent as efficient as laboratory sparks, the earth could have become covered in a dense layer of organic molecules, to a depth of 1 metre, during a period of only 10 million years. No doubt, most of these decomposed again. But a lot would have dissolved in lakes and oceans – then free from salt, which had not yet been washed out of the rocks – to form a mixture much like a thin soup.

There are other signs that the first step was easy. Radio-astronomers have discovered that the great clouds of gas which permeate the galaxy contain, in addition to the hydrogen that makes them 'reducing', many other kinds of molecules, including some biologically important ones as methyl alcohol and formaldehyde. There are also certain kinds of carbon-bearing meteorites which fall to earth from time to time and it has now been clearly proved that these have brought with themselves, from space, many compounds such as alcohols, sugars and amino-acids. This of course raises the question of whether life was implanted on earth from somewhere else, carried here in a meteorite. This is interesting but does not help us much since it could still leave us with the problem of how life started 'somewhere else'. But it seems an unnecessary line of speculation because the kinds of simple organic molecule that could survive long journeys in space could quite easily, as we have seen, be made on earth by our local processes. On the whole, it seems better to regard it as evidence, not for life outside the earth, but for the ease with which the organic molecules necessary to life can be made by non-biological means.

It is particularly striking that the molecular components of living things should form so easily and abundantly when a reducing mixture of gases, derived from hydrogen, oxygen, carbon and nitrogen, is bombarded with radiation. Life has been built, not from molecular rarities, but the most common organic molecules formed naturally under such conditions; from the nearest things to hand, in fact.

Life before Cells

But we are as yet a long way from the first cell. And from this point onwards, nature's chemical virtuosity rapidly outstrips our laboratory skills – and perhaps also our imaginations – so that until we pick up the trail again, at the first fossil record some hundreds of millions of years onwards, we have to cross a dark age in the history of life. What we can do is, not so much to seek the actual path through it, as to see whether scientifically sound paths were possible.

First, a simple point. As Darwin had already realised in an early speculation, the primeval soup could not be devoured or 'go bad' since there were no organisms then to do that. But such molecules are not permanently stable and would eventually break down by themselves. We have thus to picture this soup existing in a fairly constant condition, with the steady influx of new molecules washed down into it from the atmosphere, being balanced by the spontaneous breakdown of those already there. For many long centuries it must have been like this, with very little else happening, chemically.

There would have been a few changes, nevertheless. The evaporation of shallow waters would have led to thick soups, perhaps even crusty deposits. Elsewhere, freezing would have concentrated the molecules into the narrow channels between ice crystals. In such ways as these, some molecules would have been given a chance to join together. Bernal suggested that the surfaces of clays, which are generally attractive to molecules, may have served as catalysing sites on which they could turn into polymers. Katchalsky has strikingly endorsed this by showing that montmorillite, a common clay, is very effective in enabling amino-acids to link together into long chains. Polymers made this way on the ancient earth, while chemically and physically almost exactly the same, were of course *not* proteins. Made by blind chance in a lifeless world they were, biologically, just strings of atoms, signifying nothing.

Nucleic acids would have been much less easily made by such means, because several different steps are involved. But there are minerals such as apatite which provide attractive sites for nucleotides, and there are simple molecules such as urea which catalyse the union of phosphates and nucleotides; so that short lengths of primitive nucleic acids could have been slowly made. Even though of initially meaningless sequences, they would be true 'nucleic acids' – provided they were chemically correct, of course – since they would have the crucial ability to *replicate*. There were of course no enzymes then to help this process along, but recent experiments with artificial nucleotide polymers have shown that these will, by themselves, act as templates for replication. Strands of 'poly-U', in which the nucleotide side-groups are all of the same U type, cause unit molecules of the A type to join up into polymers; and strands of poly-C do the same for unit molecules of G type. The Watson-Crick rules are obeyed in these 'test-tube' reactions.

We suppose then that, once formed, the primitive nucleic acids would have made complementary copies of themselves, by lining up nearby nucleotide molecules, perhaps on grains of minerals or near little clumps of amino-acid polymers. It is also probable that molecules of ATP took part, from a very early stage, in all these polymerisation and replication processes, supplying the necessary energy and helping to stabilise the resulting chains, in the watery soup.

The course was then set for natural selection, evolution and life. As the primitive fragments of nucleic acid multiplied through the generations, the advantage would go to those that multiplied fastest. Eventually they would make up practically the entire population. The rate of copying would depend on the length and sequence of a chain. If a mutation occurred which changed the rate, the new strain would either grow faster and eventually 'take over', or slower and become extinct. In this very simple way, the sequences would gradually become no longer arbitrary, but significant – those which allowed fastest multiplication in that particular environment.

Some of these early nucleic acid molecules would undoubtedly have met amino-acid polymers. Evidently in some cases there was an affinity, initially of an elementary chemical nature, which gradually evolved into a *symbiosis* between them. We do not know the original basis of this. Perhaps the nucleic acids were better protected from disintegration when surrounded by amino-acids. Perhaps the amino-acids helped to prise open the ends of double strands, which made it easier for complementary new strands to grow along the open ends. But, out of all the many varieties of nucleic acid and amino-acid chains, at that time, there must have been some combinations that favoured faster reproduction and an enhanced production of those nucleic acids which had an affinity for certain amino-acid sequences. And in this way natural selection could begin also to select some amino-acid polymers, doing it indirectly through the multiplication of their related nucleic acids. Those amino-acid polymers that helped faster reproduction were themselves synthesised a little faster. Although very imperfectly copied at this stage, and barely different from those formed by blind chance, they nevertheless began to be slightly biased in their sequences by the influence of selected nucleic acids. They were beginning, by natural selection, to become *proteins*.

There were at this stage all the ingredients and processes, at their irreducible minimum, for life: self-reproducing nucleic acids, helped in their multiplication by crude proteins whose synthesis they influenced; subject to mutations; and multiplying in competition with others of their kind for the nutrients in the soup. Everything was there to enable natural selection slowly, but inexorably, to ratchet life up, notch by notch, from molecules to men.

But it was still a long way even to the first cells. The primitive symbiosis between nucleic acids and proteins had to sharpen itself into the sophisticated genetic code; the protein had to specialise and elaborate into efficient and highly discriminating enzymes; the nucleic acid had to evolve into long chains, carrying the information to determine such subtle molecules. Moreover, the nucleo-protein complexes at this stage were, in industrial language, still only 'assembly shops', not yet 'component manufacturers'. They had to develop a metabolic ability, to enable them to use simple molecules such as sugar, ammonia, carbon dioxide, etc., as sources of energy and as raw materials for constructing their own nucleotides and amino-acids. As they became more complex it would be increasingly advantageous to corral these valuable manufacturing facilities together, in a bag which would admit and even actively pump in the simple feedstock molecules.

A formidable list of evolutionary advances; but there was also a lot of time and a rich soup. Bacteria can reproduce in about 20 minutes. The early molecular complexes should have been able to go much faster than this, certainly once the proteins possessed good enzymatic properties, but even going at less than half the bacterial speed they could have produced a million million generations in a hundred million years. Recent experiments by Spiegelman have shown that RNA molecules replicate rapidly in a test-tube of soup, with a suitable enzyme present, and, moreover, quickly react to an environmental challenge – e.g. the introduction of a drug which upsets the replication process – by mutation and natural selection of new strains better adapted to the new conditions.

Vital Inventions

The first cells, rather like today's bacteria and blue-green algae, were very small individual organisms, simple by the standards of modern highly developed ones, although incredibly complex compared with anything man-made. They were *prokaryotes*, meaning that their chromosomes floated loosely in the cell, and they multiplied by a process of fission without the spectacular events of mitosis. They were scavengers, living off chemical energy extracted from energy-rich molecules in the soup by the relatively wasteful *anaerobic* (i.e. oxygen-less) processes of fermentation. While at first they lived easily on the abundant nutrients laid down in the soup by a bountiful nature during millions of years earlier – just as we now live off fossil fuels – a limit to their numbers was eventually set through the rate at which new energy-rich molecules were being made, by the ultra-violet rays and lightning strokes rending the atmosphere above, and washed down by rain into their waters.

This phase may have lasted for about 1000 million years, until the greatest of all natural inventions occurred: some cells became able to extract their energy directly from sunlight. There is clear evidence from fossils that blue-green algae could do this 2000 million years ago, as well as 'fix' their own nitrogen chemically. *Photosynthesis* had arrived and it brought the first population explosion.

It also brought the first poisonous pollution of the planet – the gas *oxygen*, released into the seas and atmosphere as a by-product of photosynthesis. There is evidence of atmospheric oxygen in rocks 1800 million years old. The early organisms were in danger of choking in their own exhaust gas. Some survived by sequestering themselves away from sun and air, where their anaerobic descendants are found today. Others found ways of neutralising oxygen by combining it with their other waste products and they eventually made a virtue out of necessity by using this energy of incinerated waste to augment their own energy supplies. This was the second great invention, the audacious adaptation of a poison into the very breath of life itself; the beginning of *respiration*, which greatly increased the availability of energy and set off another population explosion.

This probably happened between 2000 million and 1500 million years ago and it opened the way to several other developments. Mitochondria were evolved, to use the oxygen to extract energy from foods and to store it by synthesising ATP. By about 1500 million years ago, according to the fossils, the first *eukaryotic* type of cell, larger, with a clear nucleus, with other well-developed 'organs' – called *organelles* – such as mitochondria, and dividing by mitosis, had evolved. Some of these organelles are quite similar to pro-karyotic cells and it is possible that eukaryotic cells developed from small colonies of prokaryotic ones living together symbiotically, gradually specialising into organelles and becoming enclosed in a collective membrane.

There were other major developments. About 1200 million years ago the separate plant and animal kingdoms began to diverge. Fossils show that by 900 million years ago sexual reproduction had started; and that the first multi-celled organisms existed 700 million years ago. And during all this time oxygen was building up in the atmosphere, gradually changing it from 'reducing' to 'oxidising'. But the real explosion into a variety of living things, the 'radiation of species', did not come until the beginning of the Cambrian period, about 600 million years ago. Before then, the population was biologically rather monotonous, consisting largely of photosynthetic plankton. It is possible that the new step was the development of *eating* by some organisms, ancestors of the *carnivores*, beginning with feeding on small bacteria and then moving on to the larger eukaryotic cells. As we saw in chapter 9, foraging is an advanced activity which is obviously a spur to multi-cellular development, and predation is a spur to the diversification of species.

The Great Ages

Life in water developed richly during the Cambrian period. Amoeba, algae, jelly-fish, sponges, sea-lilies, sea-anemones, corals, marine worms, and starfish flourished. There were shellfish, the forebears of modern oysters, mussels and snails; and other molluscs, the ancient relatives of the octopus, squid, cuttlefish and nautilus. Above all there were the *trilobites*, rather like the wood-louse in appearance, body and numerous limbs encased in jointed armour, in hundreds of varieties from half a centimetre up to half a metre long. They eventually became extinct, but their type of body structure has been inherited by three-quarters of today's animal species, including the spiders, winged insects, mites, millipedes, crabs and lobsters, as well as the formidable large water scorpions of 350 million years ago. This general class of creatures, with bodies and limbs encased in hard jointed coats, was also the first to achieve air-breathing and flying.

Sizeable creatures need some support for their bodies, either of the above kind or an *internal skeleton* – a jointed *backbone* in fact, with ribs and limb bones. We know little of the oldest, probably pre-Cambrian, ancestors of backboned creatures, but the development probably began as a stiffening tube – the *notochord* – something like a minute thin resilient sausage. The embryo of the modern backboned animal has one, running the length of its body and, as the infant develops, the backbone vertebrae gradually grow in its place. Traces of backboned creatures 450 million years old have been found, and complete skulls and skeletons of specimens about 10 to 20 cm. long show that several species were abundant 350 million years ago. They were like fish, but armoured in thick plates of bone – which they needed, having to live with the water scorpions – and a solid layer of bone armour round the head, the origin of our skull. They had no jaws, only a small hole for the mouth, and lived by grubbing in the mud at the bottom of ponds and streams. Later they grew bigger and faster, and moved into the sea, where they presumably found refuge from the water scorpions. Gradually they lost their body armour, although the bone head remained, and became true fishes. The developments of biting jaws and paired fins were very important, the first to enable them to become predators, the second to give them skilful movement and balance in the water. With paired fins, their torpedo-like bodies became symmetrical, the left-hand and right-hand sides being generally mirror images of each other. This also is something that we and all the other back-boned animals owe to them.

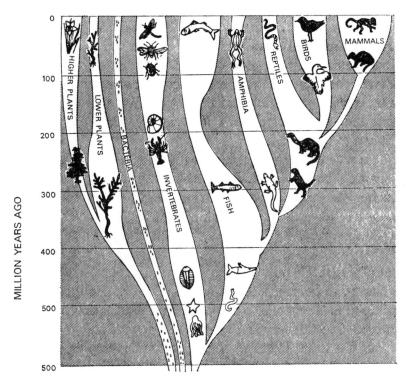

Evolutionary tree.

During this *Age of Fishes*, over the next 50 million years, a great step was taken in a different direction. Plants became adapted to land. This was a difficult change, because they had then to get water from the ground, which led to the evolution of roots; it had to be storable; and it had to be piped round the plant, through the fibrous woody tissue also developed to hold them up. But long centuries in swampy ground, which must often have dried out, would clearly have guided this phase of evolution. The chlorophyll parts obviously gained by being above water, just as the water-gathering parts gained by spreading deep into moist mud.

Suddenly, the world was into the *Carboniferous Age*, beginning about 300 million years ago. Vast stretches of swampy land became densely forested with great ferns, horsetail trees and other plants. These flourished in millions during the next 80 million years and, falling into the swamps, laid down today's great coal deposits. Land plants with true leaves, roots and stems became common. Eventually *seeds* were developed, which had the great advantage over spores that they could wait, years if necessary, for the right conditions to germinate.

Animals quickly spread on to the land, once plant food became plentiful there. No doubt, long periods of difficulty during dry spells in streams, ponds, and swamps had bred creatures able to endure without water, rather as today's lungfish survive by burrowing into mud and breathing air. There were also crabs on the seashore living half in and half out of water. The jointed-armour creatures led the migration, going on to become spiders, land scorpions, centipedes, and millipedes. There were also some spectacular developments such as dragon-flies with wings 1 metre across.

But the fishes followed closely, some developing into the first *amphibians*, the direct ancestors of today's newts, frogs, and salamanders. It is probable that early backboned fish had both gills for breathing and an air bladder as well, partly to hold them up in the water, as in today's fish, and partly to enable them to breathe air when trapped in stagnant pools or mud flats. They also had two pairs of fins beneath their bodies, fore and aft, set in strong muscular lobes, and could crawl about a bit on these, when stranded. In some strains the lobes gradually evolved into limbs and the air bladders into lungs. These amphibians, like fish, laid and fertilised their eggs in water, which spawned into tadpole-like infants, breathing at first in water through skin and gills, and then later developing lungs and legs. And so here began the great group of four-limbed creatures, with ears evolved from gills, which includes the backboned land animals and birds, as well as ourselves.

The amphibians in the end failed to conquer the land – and today are one of the minor classes – because they still depended on water for spawning. The great invention which fully liberated the backboned animals from water was the large egg, able to be laid on land, protected by a shell, with a membrane to prevent it drying out, and containing a large supply of food and fluid which would nourish the growing embryo up to the stage where it could hatch out like a small adult, fairly well able to look after itself. It also became essential of course for such eggs to be fertilised before they were laid. These great developments, which probably started in the Carboniferous Age with a primitive amphibian similar to a lizard, reached their climax about 200 million years ago in the *Age of Reptiles*. These creatures ruled the earth for many millions of years as the *dinosaurs*, such as the gigantic tyrannosaurus, the aquatic brontosaurus, and the flying pterodactyl, but today their only close relatives are the lizards, snakes, turtles, tortoises and crocodiles.

This was also a time of other changes. The great class of *birds* started from a lizard-like climbing reptile, whose scales gradually evolved into feathers. Plants began to *flower*, with a strong symbiosis developed between themselves and the insects. They benefited from the insects carrying their pollen and these in turn thrived on their nectar. But, for us at least, the most significant of all developments was something quite different, which began very early during the age of reptiles and continued quietly all through that period.

Inconspicuously, from a lizard-like branch of the reptiles, there evolved small shrew-like creatures. They must have lived modestly, eating insects, worms and eggs, hiding in the undergrowth from the dinosaurs, perhaps dwelling in trees and nocturnal in habit. But they had enormous potentialities. They were warm-blooded and fur-covered, which enabled them to hold their internal temperatures constant at a high level, suitable for active life, unlike the reptiles and insects which become inert and helpless in cold weather. They also had – as the birds would have – a four-chambered heart and a bigger brain. And they gave milk to their young, which in most cases were born as infants rather than hatched from eggs. With the suckling of their offspring by these *mammals*, family life began.

The *Cretaceous* era, beginning about 140 million years ago, brought settled warm climates and an abundance of life, especially the *ammonites*, molluscs whose spiral shells are the most familiar of all fossils; and the great chalk deposits were built up from the bodies of innumerable creatures and plants. This long historical summer came to an end about 80 million years ago, with drastic changes during which the dinosaurs became extinct – perhaps killed by cold – as well as the ammonites, leaving the earth mainly to the mammals, birds, insects and fishes. By 70 million years ago, when another warm period began, plants and animals were becoming fairly similar to today's. Almost all the present species of insects had arrived, including the social ones. Many fish, such as trout, were essentially modern.

Even before then, 90 million years ago, the mammals were beginning to split up into their main branches, including our own distinct order of *primates*. There were two broad groups of mammals: the *marsupials*, such as kangaroos and wombats, who carried their young while very small in external pouches; and the much larger class of those who carried them to a more fully grown stage in *placenta* in their mothers' bodies, a development which started among the small insect-eating shrews, moles and hedgehogs. By 35 million years ago, early rodents, horses, pigs and monkeys had arrived. Some mammals had gone back to sea, to evolve into today's whales and dolphins, while others learned to fly, as today's bats. And about 30 million years ago, man himself began to diverge from the other apes.

This second historical summer also ended abruptly, with the ice ages of nearly 1 million years ago. Again, there were profound effects on all kinds of life, even though most were much more resilient by this time. Nevertheless some, such as the sabre-toothed tiger, became extinct and there were other temporary developments such as the mammoths, long-haired relatives of the elephant, and the woolly rhinoceros. But the ice ages set the stage for yet another Age, that of man.

Ancestors of Man

The primates started at least 70 million years ago from creatures rather like tree-shrews. Living in trees, jumping from branch to branch, they needed good eyesight, as well as hands that could grasp things between fingers and thumb. Above all, they needed more brain to compute their high-level and high-speed acrobatics safely and surely. Expansion of the brain is the key evolutionary feature of the primates. Necessary first for their manoeuvres in trees, it enabled them later to live by their wits rather than by physical prowess. Family life also developed and fewer offspring were produced but with a better individual chance of survival. The line continued through small creatures like lemurs and tarsiers, to the monkeys and great apes – of which the gorilla and chimpanzee are the nearest modern relatives to man – able to use sticks and other things as primitive weapons and implements.

By about 30 million years ago there were already apes

showing slightly human features; and there is evidence going back 14 million years of a type known as *Ramapithecus*, found in India and Africa, sufficiently human as to be no longer surely classed as an ape. So many of the key evolutions of the primates along the line to man have been found in south and east Africa that there is a good possibility of Darwin's suggestion, that man evolved in Africa, being correct. Another major discovery was the type known as *Australopithecus*, recently dated back some 2.6 million years by Richard Leakey who has also discovered a skull of another manlike creature, alive at about the same time, with a brain of 800 c.c. volume. While still well below today's size (about 1500 c.c.) it is much beyond that of the largest living apes (500 c.c.).

The next step was *Homo erectus*, examples of which are the *Java man* and the *Pekin man*, with a brain of about 1000 c.c. and limbs much like today's, a toolmaker who hunted deer and cooked it on fire hearths in his caves. Probably about a million years ago he began to diverge into two branches, *Neanderthal* and *Cro-Magnon* man. The Neanderthaler appeared about 150,000 years ago, before the last ice age, with a large skull and upright walk. He had better weapons and hunting tools, probably clothed himself in animal skins, and revered his dead, burying them in flower-strewn graves.

But before the end of the last ice age he had become extinct, unable to stand up to the Cro-Magnon man who swept through Europe about 40,000 years ago, probably from Asia. This was *Homo sapiens*, having a brain of full modern size, tall and upright, with a flat face and high forehead, looking much like a modern European. By the end of the last glacial period, 10,000 years ago, his cave paintings had become highly skilful and stylish. Those times of bitterly cold weather also bred in Europe a race of Eskimo-like people whose culture suggests an affinity with the modern Eskimo. Prehistoric man, driven by the vagaries of the times, was a great intercontinental traveller. Quite apart from the arctic climates which so frequently challenged him, food was a constant problem. For the 2 to 3 million years of his existence as a scavenger and hunter, this must have kept his world numbers down to at most a few million. Only when he learned to domesticate plants and animals, about 10,000 years ago, could the human race begin to grow vastly.

Life in the Universe

If nature's laws have brought life from matter, through replication, mutation, and natural selection, then perhaps they have done so at other places in the universe. Wherever the materials and conditions for it exist, then surely, in time, life must evolve? At present we have no evidence for life elsewhere in the universe. Admittedly, it is quite certain that the first step on the road to life – the formation of the elementary molecules from which our kind of living matter is made – is an easy one which occurs extensively throughout our own galaxy. But it is only a first step and all we can do at present is to consider the chances of conditions existing which would permit the many other steps to follow it.

In the solar system the most obvious other place for life is Mars, although it is not by our standards very promising, with its desert-red rocks, dust storms, moon-like craters, and temperatures which at best are comparable with those of our antarctic. Its white polar caps are now known to be solid carbon dioxide. But it does have an atmosphere – very thin, mainly carbon dioxide, some carbon monoxide, practically no oxygen, water vapour, or nitrogen – and when a laboratory imitation of it was exposed to ultra-violet rays, some organic compounds were formed. Water is of course essential to life as we know it. While Mars is now pretty dry there is clear evidence that water ran freely on it in geologically recent times. Dried-up river beds have been photographed and many of the surface rocks contain chemically-combined water, which presumably living organisms could have learned to extract, if necessary. Whether there is enough nitrogen in the rocks as nitrates, or whether Martian life could have managed to use the very small amounts in the atmosphere, we do not know, but this is probably the most critical factor concerning life on Mars. It may of course be that life has evolved and then gone underground, where there could be free water and mineral nutrients. Space probes should be able to answer some of these questions in the next few years.

Looking beyond the solar system, the indications from the general processes of star formation are that it should be rather common for stars to have planets. It is also hard to see how a star could cope with all the angular momentum, which must have been present in its parent swirl of interstellar gas cloud, unless this angular momentum were mainly taken up in a set of planets round it. Astronomers in fact now generally consider that planets must be very numerous; and that there may be as many as 1000 million similar to the earth in our own galaxy. If this is so, then life almost certainly exists in many places throughout the universe.

Could it have become intelligent and technically advanced? We do not know of course, but there is no firm reason to rule this out. There is little prospect, on the basis of our own technical knowledge, of making contact. The distances are so enormous, even for messages at the speed of light. The weakening of signals, spreading out radially over such huge distances, would also make communication extremely difficult, unless of course there are much more technically advanced forms of life, able to tap and control natural sources of energy on an immense scale. Perhaps, one day, a radio-astronomer here may intercept an intelligent signal passing through space. Without stepping into the realms of science fiction, it is hard to imagine a more exciting discovery than this, or one which would more profoundly affect the whole outlook of mankind.

12

Mind over Matter

Living things respond to events round them, in their own self-interest, to the best of their ability. Plants bend towards the light. The euglena swims towards it. A dog springs up suddenly at a distant sound and a cat bristles at the sight. The higher animals get news about their surroundings through several senses and respond in the way that seems best for them in the circumstances.

This requires a lot of organisation. Messages have to be collected from the eyes, ears or other senses, and orders despatched to the muscles telling them to move in complex but precise ways, often at top speed. Above all, decisions have to be made, to make the right response for the situation. Something has to be in overall charge of the machinery of the body to make it an integrated organism, able to act effectively as a whole. This of course is the task of the nervous system, which in man and the higher animals is a dense network of long thin nerve cells, the *neurons*, threading the body. The *sensory* neurons bring news into the central nervous system – the spinal cord and brain – and the *motor* neurons carry instructions out to the tissues.

A neuron has a nucleus, cytoplasm, organelles and membrane, like any other cell. But the membrane spreads outwards as a tree-like structure of short, branching fibres, its *dendrites*, which collect information for the cell. It also extends in one direction as a long thin fibre, its *axon*, by which it sends its message to another part of the body. At its far end the axon branches out into another, smaller, tree-like structure, through which the nerve delivers its message to the dendrites of another nerve or muscle cell. It does this by releasing a chemical (acetylcholine) which excites or inhibits them.

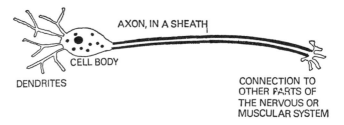

A nerve cell.

The basic signal is an electrical pulse, which travels along the axon at about 10 to 100 metres a second, according as the fibre is thin or thick. The process is extraordinary and is arranged so as to make the signal an 'all-or-none' one. Each pulse in an axon has the same size and shape, goes along at the same speed and does not fade as it travels. The information in a message is indicated, not by the individual pulse, but by the frequency with which a neuron fires successive pulses, up to a few hundred a second, along its axon. For example, there is a group of cells in the arm which fire at a different characteristic rate for each angle of the elbow, so that the brain can know the arm's position.

The neuron is said to 'fire' because a certain stimulus is needed to set it off, just as a firework fuse needs a spark to ignite, and once started the electrochemical process runs along its axon by a 'chain reaction', again as a flame runs along a burning fuse. All this is brought about by the membrane round the cell and axon, which is able to pump certain electrical ions into (or out of) the cytoplasm from the fluid outside. By means of a slight imbalance of positive and negative ions, the cytoplasm is held normally at a negative voltage, nearly a tenth of a volt below the outside, and it is kept short of sodium ions but rich in potassium ions relative to the outside. When an impulse is fired, the membrane of the cell temporarily changes its permeability, to let in a few positive sodium ions, which make the cytoplasm locally and slightly electropositive at the 'breach'; after which it lets out a few positive potassium ions, so more-or-less restoring the electrical status quo. This transient change of condition, with the ensuing inflow of sodium and outflow of potassium, runs as a pulse along the axon, like the burning zone in the fuse. After about one or two thousandths of a second, all is ready to fire again. Only a few ions are exchanged and the stock of potassium in the axon is enough for many thousands of firings. In any case, the enzyme ion pumps can maintain the nerves fully charged, provided they are supplied with energy.

Most sensory messages are sent to the spinal cord, where they typically travel up to the brain and stimulate it to send instructions back down the cord and along the motor neurons to the muscles. Many messages are not brought to the conscious attention of the 'higher' parts of the brain. They stimulate the reflex or involuntary actions and automatic skills – as when the pianist's fingers move instinctively over the keyboard, leaving his mind free to interpret his music – and they rarely penetrate beyond the *cerebellum,* one of the earliest evolved and most primitive parts of the brain.

The brain is a great sheet of nerve cells, about 10,000 million, so large that it is crinkled into numerous folds to fit into the skull. These neurons are extensively interconnected by a thick felt of threads, so that they are continually stimulating one another into activity, causing waves of phased firings to ripple repeatedly across the sheet. In its relaxed state the brain settles into a steady 'alpha rhythm' of about 10 cycles a second, which can be detected electrically through the skull. The cells are then 'ticking over', idling in unison; and ready, when called upon, to jump into the more complex patterns of activity which go with concentrated thought.

The most prominent parts of the human brain are the two *cerebral hemispheres*, on the left and right sides, connected by a bridge of nerve fibres. At their base the *brain stem* joins them to the spinal cord. Near the top end of this stem the *thalamus* region of the brain acts as a central relay station, dispatching messages to and fro between the higher brain and the rest of the nervous system. Covering the cerebral hemispheres is the *cerebral cortex*, the famous 'grey matter', an incredibly dense mat of nerves and connecting fibres, which is where the higher mental work is done and consciousness becomes possible. Various areas of it have particular responsibilities, for vision, for hearing, for various bodily movements, for speaking, and so on. The front part is used for original thinking and forward planning.

The Transfiguration

In his book *Man on His Nature*, Sherrington vividly portrayed the brain by imagining the firing impulses to be tiny points of light, some streaming in trains along the nerve fibres, others flashing like stationary beacons at the nodes where different fibres meet. To quote from it: 'Suppose we choose the hour of deep sleep. Then only in some sparse and out of the way places are nodes flashing and trains of light-points running . . . At one such place we can watch the behaviour of a group of lights perhaps a myriad strong . . . They are superintending the beating of the heart . . . The great knotted headpiece of the whole sleeping system lies for the most part dark and quite especially so the roof-brain [cerebral cortex]. Occasionally at places in it lighted points flash or move but soon subside . . . Where however the stalk [spinal cord] joins the headpiece, there goes forward in a limited field a remarkable display. A dense constellation of some thousands of nodal points burst out every few seconds into a short phase of rhythmical flashing . . . What is this doing? It manages the taking of our breath while we sleep. Should we continue to watch . . . after a time an impressive change . . . accrues. In the great head-end . . . spring up myriads of twinkling stationary lights and myriads of trains of moving lights of many different directions . . . The great topmost sheet of the mass . . . becomes now a sparkling field of rhythmic flashing points with trains of travelling sparks hurrying hither and thither. The brain is waking and with it the mind is returning . . . Swiftly the head-mass becomes an enchanted loom where millions of flashing shuttles weave a dissolving pattern . . . subpatterns of this great harmony of activity stretch down into the unlit tracks of the stalk-piece . . . Strings of flashing and travelling sparks engage the lengths of it . . . the body is up and rises to meet its waking day.'

But the deepest marvel lies even beyond this – in the simple words 'the mind is returning'. Somehow, the great constellations of flashes, in stimulating one another to their dazzling climax, bring forth something so utterly different as to seem like a new world altogether, the realm of the *conscious mind*, aware of itself. The enchanted loom does not merely weave scintillating patterns. There occurs a transfiguration which turns a biochemical masterpiece into a conscious person.

The mental world, with its pleasures and pains, hopes and fears, anticipations and motives, thoughts and plans, sensibilities and self-awareness, seems to be something entirely different from the physical world, with its space and time, atoms and molecules, inertia and gravitation, energy and momentum, particles and waves. There seems to be a complete gulf between our notions of them. In the physical world a pattern of air pressures beats on our eardrums; in the mental one we are entertained by a nightingale's song. In the physical world a well-understood chain of processes brings the news to our eyes, through their pupils, on to the retina, and takes it onwards, first photochemically and then electrochemically, to the highest centres of the brain; but at that point the physics appears to say 'goodbye', just where the mental world takes over, and we become consciously aware of the scene before us; again a transfiguration seems to take place and, out of the physical processes that stimulated it, something which seems to be utterly non-physical is created. As Sherrington has said, 'it is a far cry from an electrical reaction in the brain to suddenly seeing the world around one, with all its distances, its colours and chiaroscuro'.

The Nature of Mind

As persons, we naturally feel that some aspects of our lives are personal. Each seems to have two sides to his life, a public bodily one and a private inward one where ideas form, experience grows and feelings linger. When a patient complains to his doctor of a pain, he is reporting a feeling to which only he has direct access. His doctor may succeed in diagnosing its physical cause – if there is one – and may recollect a pain he once felt and suppose that his patient now feels similarly, but nevertheless he cannot actually *experience* his patient's pain, for this is private.

But *private* does not mean *isolated*. The alert mind is a supreme example of something 'in touch' with the outside world. It is the centre of sense and sensibility, taking in news from outside through a vast network of sensory neurons and reacting back on the world through its command of the body. We can see a long way into our companions' inner worlds simply by looking at the expressions on their faces, whether friendly, angry, worried or confident. In the hands of a Schubert, Shakespeare, or Dostoevsky, music and literature enable feelings to resonate directly between our minds. And we all *talk* to one another! We 'speak our minds'. What is a conversation, but an exchange of ideas between two or more different minds? Insofar as man has developed and uses the most expressive and articulate language, his mind is the most publicly accessible of all. We have an inkling of what goes on in the minds of the higher animals – chimpanzees, dogs, cats, dolphins – from their use of limited languages, but inscrutability sets in rapidly as we move down the line to inarticulate life. Indeed there is a good case for arguing that command of a 'language', in the most general sense of being able to give some public expression of personal experience, is the key attribute of mind. Wittgenstein, for example, said that: 'You learned the *concept* "pain" when you learned language.' Certainly, at the other extreme, the really private 'mind' appears to be no mind at all; few of us think that a stone has one.

Having a mind means, to that mind's person, having a *privileged access* to certain experiences, thoughts and feelings. Descartes said 'I think, therefore I am', which is a fair point provided that it is not exaggerated into the view that mind can exist without body (or brain) or that there is no mind but one's own. The experiences of different persons differ essentially not in their privacy but their accessibility. One's own mental experiences cannot be observed through any of the bodily organs of sense. They are already there, in one's own mind. They are *first-hand* experiences and, as such, have an impregnable personal reality about them. Someone else's mental experiences we never know directly, only at *second-hand*, by looking at his face, watching his movements or listening to him. Because they come to us only through intermediate, physical, channels a minor act of faith is needed to believe in their reality.

The most privileged *knowledge* we have is that of our own conscious decisions. Aristotle defined man as a *choosing* creature, someone who makes autonomous decisions aimed at long-term goals selected by himself. Of all the knowledge one has, the knowledge of what one has decided to do is the most purely personal. It is knowledge which, because it originates in the person making the decision, has not been learnt. Freedom of choice means that the outputs are not completely determined by the inputs; the response may be influenced by *memories*, for example, or by adherence to long-term goals. An amusing though false analogy is that of a familiar machine – such as an old motor car – which, because of looseness in its joints or other uncertainties, does not always respond in the way we ask of it and so has a 'personality'.

Although the mind, unlike the brain, cannot be measured with physical instruments, it can nevertheless be studied in its own terms, at both first- and second-hand. At first-hand each of us looks at his own mind by introspection or self-reflection – and there are some fascinating accounts by musicians, mathematicians, scientists, etc., of how their ideas came to them – but this is so quintessentially subjective that we can learn little, scientifically, this way except for one key thing: each of us knows at first-hand that his own mind exists. This protects us from falling into the trap of supposing that the physiological story of the brain is all that there is or that living things are no more than input-output machines or automata.

Of course, when we turn to second-hand knowledge of the mind, gained by studying the physically expressed activities of minds other than our own, as in experimental *psychology*, it is often a useful tactic to regard the mind under study as a 'black box' for the purpose of measuring and correlating its responses to standard stimuli; how quickly it reacts, for example, to a sudden change of light. Indeed, such *behaviouristic* studies can be useful practically – for example, in determining the best time settings of road traffic lights – but because they stand at arm's length from the mental processes themselves, they cannot throw much light on the nature of mind.

It may be possible to get closer by studying, second-hand, the *creative* performance of the mind. The most interesting recent examples are studies of how people use *language*. In their everyday conversations and compositions, people use language creatively, constructing original sentences. Words are chosen, ordered into various groups, and structured into principal and subsidiary clauses to make complete sentences which, in the more complex examples, are quite original.

Chomsky has emphasised how remarkable this is. A modern language such as English is an enormous hotch-potch of unsystematic rules, cutting across and countermanding one another in the most complex ways. To take a simple example of Chomsky's, consider the sentence 'The dog in the corner is hungry' and turn it into a question. It becomes 'Is the dog in the corner hungry?' But what is the general rule for this change? It is not just a matter of moving 'is' to the front, for this could lead to disaster with the similar sentence 'The dog that is in the corner is hungry'. The rule in fact involves the deep structure of the sentence, since the whole phrase 'The dog [that is] in the corner' acts as a single noun subject.

By many such examples Chomsky reminds us that everyday language, as an intellectual structure, is extremely complex and intricate. Much more so than, say, Euclid's geometry, or perhaps even modern physics. Yet a child in junior school speaks it with ease, showing a fluency, instinctive ability, and instant creativity that could, if it were say chess, music, or mathematics, mark him as a genius. Indeed we might wonder what early inhibition prevents most of us, except a rare Mozart or Gauss, from equalling in these fields our ability in our own language. Moreover, the child does not in general even know, except intuitively, the great mass of interlocking rules of which he is such a master. He has picked up the facility from parents who usually have not even tried, other than casually and amateurishly – generally not knowing explicitly more than a few rules themselves – to teach him how to construct sentences.

Chomsky therefore argues in effect that the young child's

output of grammatical constructions is so enormous, compared with the fragmentary input, that his ability to manipulate grammar must be inbuilt. Moreover it must be a knowledge of *universal* grammar that he has – some very broad and abstract rules of logical construction – since Japanese comes out as easily in Japan as English does in England. Chomsky is thus led to the view that the unconscious levels of the mind, which Freud first postulated, contain instinctive knowledge of certain logical 'structures' or self-evident truths, including the underlying rules of all language.

There are physiological parallels for this. What the eye takes in, for example, is not sent direct to the brain as raw data. It is processed on the way, to pick out significant abstract features such as contrasts of intensity, presence of straight lines, corners and ends of lines; and various cells in the brain respond to these particular abstract features. Since we think geometrically most easily in terms of straight lines, it is striking to find that the 'visual' neurons in the brain are particularly arranged in patterns suitable for handling data processed into parallel straight lines.

Again, for medical reasons it is sometimes necessary, by cutting the bridging nerves, to bisect the two hemispheres of the brain into 'two brains'. Both can then learn and behave in the normal way, but only one of them holds speech areas of the original brain, which are laid down at an early stage in the development of the foetus. It is then found that the self-consciousness of someone with a bisected brain is linked only to the events in his linguistic hemisphere. When precautions are taken to prevent one side of his body from communicating with the other, it is possible to get in touch with him normally through the linguistic hemisphere, but not through the other.

It may then be that the human mind is a result of the evolution of a genetic code for the construction of the linguistic areas of the brain. Is *mind* some kind of collective performance of certain very intricate atomic structures, working according to the laws of physics? We know of other collective effects of atoms, not possessed by them individually, such as heat and sound, but it may be an impertinence to mention them in the same context as mind. But we have no idea at all of how matter, by physical laws, could exhibit the characteristics of mind. Certainly the laws of physics give no inkling of this. But it would be rash to suppose that we now know all or even many of the laws of nature. Like psychology and physiology today, chemistry and physics seemed separated by an unbridgeable gap a century ago; but atomic physics and the quantum theory have since brought them together as a common understanding.

Complementarity

The world of matter, from particles and quanta to cells and neurons; the world of the mind, from ideas and words to experiences and feelings; it seems impossible to unite them as one understanding. Yet they are linked through and through. Even this book is a scrap of matter expressly constructed to carry ideas from one mind to another. Loss of brain produces loss of mind. A brain tumour may cause mental disorder. Worrying thoughts can provoke physiological disturbances. In neurosurgery, when the brain of a conscious patient is probed in certain places, by an electrode, the patient relives in his mind various personal experiences. Certain brain operations (pre-frontal leucotomy) change the personality. And there is now clear evidence that mental experiences in infancy, such as the 'imprinting' process by which ducklings and chicks learn to follow their mother, physically change the brain cells, both in their RNA content and in the pattern of their interconnections.

By showing these close links between mind and brain, modern science has sharpened the age-old philosophical dilemma of the relation between mind and matter. These seem utterly different, yet are closely linked. How can this be? Has nature set any other riddles of such a kind? Yes: in chapter 7 we saw that particle properties and wave properties, which seem irreconcilably different, both turn up in the same elementary pieces of matter. And we saw how this could be resolved, through Bohr's complementarity principle, by concluding that elementary matter is neither waves nor particles, but something which, when we examine it, we cannot avoid distorting into looking like one or the other. This stems from the nature of Planck's constant, by which a subjective element is unavoidably embedded in our observations of nature. What we see depends on our point of view and nature does not allow us a single all-seeing viewpoint.

There is perhaps some comfort in this for the mind-matter problem. It is scarcely believable that classical philosophy, subtly analysing primitive ideas of time, space and matter, could have deduced the extraordinary concepts of wave-particle duality. These were forced on us by the hard facts of experimental physics; and modern philosophy has had to make the best accommodation with them that it could. We now face the even more extraordinary duality of mind and matter; and because each of these seems incomprehensible when considered in terms of the other, classical philosophy has been tempted to argue that one or other of them may be an illusion. But it could be that the problem is another result of our limited, subjective, way of looking at things; and that, one day, mind and matter may become conceptually joined, even if not 'understood', in some common scheme unified by its own 'Planck's constant' or 'complementarity principle'. In fact, the idea of complementarity originated from psychology, when William James (*Principles of Psychology*, 1890) used it to discuss effects of split personality. Bohr took it up, made it the cornerstone of his understanding of wave-particle dualism, and also foresaw the possibility of its application to the mind-matter problem, as has been done recently by Globus (*Science*, 15 June, 1973).

Each of us, in principle at least, can make either a subjective enquiry, looking introspectively at his own mental
events to which he has direct access; or an objective one,
using instruments and probes to look from the outside at a
brain as an object of scientific study, including even his own
brain if he cares to peer at it through, say, a closed-circuit
television system. Introspectively, he experiences his mental
events and can, if he wishes, believe that to each one there
is a corresponding neural event in his brain, but he cannot
observe these neural events because, *so far as his purely subjective enquiries are concerned*, his neurons are invisible and
silent channels of news flowing in through them from the
objective world outside. This is news which acted in the first
place on his senses physically – through photons and sound
waves, etc. – and therefore is evidence of an external world
of matter. But his awareness of that news occurs through
experiences within his mind, and therefore is evidence of a
world of mind. And because, as a purely subjective observer,
he can never know that these mental events are neural
events – since his neurons are in themselves invisible and
silent to him – he can argue on his evidence that mind and
matter are *distinct* realities.

Alternatively, he can be an objective observer, looking
at living brains through his apparatus and at the same time
asking their owners questions. From this he discovers that
what they say about their mental events, as well as their
actions, corresponds strikingly with their physical neural
events. He can thus argue on this evidence that matter is
objective and real, and that mind is merely a name for
certain performances of a brain.

What he cannot do is to enquire both subjectively and
objectively *at the same time*, even by the trick of watching
his own brain on the television screen. For he cannot watch
all his events because the news of what is on the screen must,
in his nerves and brain, stimulate more neural events while
on its way to becoming an image in his mind. He can never

fully observe the neural events which carry news to his own mind – neither subjectively, because his own neurons are invisible and silent carriers of news external to them; nor objectively, because the very attempt to observe them changes them – although in principle there is nothing to prevent him objectively observing someone else's neurons at work.

We see then, as Globus has emphasised, that because none of us can be both inside and outside his own neural network, there is a fundamental limitation in our powers of observation. Inside our own network we know our own mental events directly but cannot sense our own neural processes. Looking out at someone else's network we can watch his neural processes but only, at best, infer his mental ones. There is a complementarity between the two points of view. We can switch from one to the other but this changes the face of the mind-matter duality which nature presents to us. A complete account calls for both faces but these cannot be fused into a single portrait because each excludes the other. It is remarkably like wave-particle duality and Bohr's complementarity principle.

13

Man and Nature

In Our Place

We live on a small planet of an ordinary star, in a suburb of a common type of galaxy, one of billions spread everywhere in all directions throughout an enormous bowl of space. It is likely that, in a single creative event, more than a million times farther back than the dawn of civilisation, the universe exploded out of a fireball of hydrogen. The galaxies condensed from this primordial matter and are still being swept increasingly apart by the very expansion of space itself. Whether everything will eventually fall together again, to relive backwards its earliest fiery moments, or instead go on spreading outwards for ever, so clearing our skies of other galaxies, we do not know; nor even whether we shall be swallowed up ignominiously one day by a nearby black hole.

A picture of breathtaking grandeur, but hardly one to inflate our ideas about the place of man in nature. Even life itself seems reduced to a mere chemical extravaganza, an exuberant outcome of molecules acting as patterns for the formation of others; and of chance molecular accidents – mutations – enabling some kinds to become copied faster than others, so giving them the edge in natural selection. And, while our own life is sandwiched in the thin film of air and water which separates a small ball of rock from the void of space, it seems increasingly likely that there is other life, some perhaps even highly advanced, in the universe.

But there is another side to the picture. This far-reaching

knowledge of nature has reached individual human minds through personal experiences and then been contributed to the pool of common human understanding. It is our telescopes and microscopes that have sought information from the depths of the universe and unravelled the finest matter; and our minds that have made a coherent picture of it all. Even where nature has forbidden a visual picture, as in the wave-particle duality, we have still been able to forge an extremely effective quantum calculus for analysing most subtle aspects of matter and motion.

The portrait of nature, then, is *our* picture. Whether it *really* is nature that we see in it is an idle speculation, for the world of this picture is the only objective one we know. But because it is our picture, painted by science, like all portraits it carries the tell-tale marks of its painter overlaying those of its subject. And by looking at these we can bring the picture into a closer relationship with ourselves.

Choice, Chance and Purpose

To primitive man, terrified by thunder and lightning, earth-quakes and eclipses, bewildered by vagaries of the climate, possessed by infirmities and afflictions, denied the comfort of any understanding of the things around him, the world must have appeared a plaything of capricious gods and demons. The few things that behaved regularly – the rising and setting of sun and moon, the straightness of a shaft of sunlight, the fall of things to the earth – must have nursed his sanity through those dark ages of incomprehensible terrors. No wonder that astronomy, geometry and mechanics became the first exact sciences.

But, since Galileo and Newton, the pendulum has swung far the other side, towards a deterministic picture of nature. We confidently turn to calendars and almanacs for the times of the next full moon, or high tide, or eclipse. We may still rail against the gods when our affairs go wrong, but only as a histrionic gesture. Pushed to its limit, however, determinism means that the course of every atom of the world today is set precisely by all that has gone before; that, for example, the fine details of the primeval big bang have predetermined exactly the flow of pen and ink now writing these words. Absurd, yes, but philosophy has been troubled for centuries with determinism and the fatalism and predestination linked with it. What happens then to freewill and our moral responsibility for personal action? Irrespective of whether I make one choice, rather than another, out of actual preference or mere indifference, the fact is that, if every atom of my body is moved according to a preset programme, then I am a mere passive spectator of its actions and it is a delusion that I am in control.

Nature, however, is not exactly deterministic. Even classical mechanics left a loophole. Consider a ball rolling down a smooth valley which very gradually and symmetrically opens out into two valleys separated by a sharp ridge. The ball goes down one or the other. In the limit, its motion at the branch point is not deterministic. The argument goes differently when we take atomicity into account, which limits the smoothness of such motions. Classical determinism assumed that perfectly exact motions are possible and that, in principle at least, they can be known precisely, but the quantum of action has put an end to all that. Nature does not have the exactitude that materialistic arguments against freewill and personal responsibility assumed.

The symbol for nature is no longer a piece of clockwork but a roulette wheel. Chance is king but its subjects, the elementary particles, are so small and many that we rarely perceive its effects directly. An electron or other particle has some inherent latitude in its motion but when large numbers go through the same situation they scatter in a well-determined pattern, so that we see nature in the large as a regular world of cause and effect; a picture on the television screen or rainbow in the sky.

There is also the regularity, coming from large numbers of chance movements, which underlies the second law of thermodynamics. We start with a very uneven distribution of particles – a heap of sand on a tray for example – and find that their chance movements – brought about by shaking the tray – bring them invariably into more evenly spread distributions. The sun shines, not because of any physical repulsion of photons from it, but simply because it is a prolific generator of photons moving randomly in all directions, inwards and outwards.

The ultimate source of heaped-up distributions is the early universe itself, a special structure with particles streaming apart and increasing their gravitational potential energy, from which all subsequent special structures, the galaxies, the sun and earth, ourselves, have been formed. The energy from the big bang is still flowing through all the veins of the universe, bursting out in all kinds of special structures. The chance of a large special structure, such as a meteoric crater on the moon or a footprint in the sand, being made by a fortuitous, undirected rearrangement of the particles is so incredibly small that such a structure in practice is always created by the external intervention of a splash of the ordered energy still rebounding round the universe from the big bang, whether embodied in the kinetic energy of the meteorite that crashed into the moon or in the biological energy of the man that walked along the beach, or in some other form.

Once such a structure is made, the chance effects that smooth away unusual distributions can get to work on it and gradually wear it down to the undifferentiated background once more. And so the histories of such structures are unsymmetrical in time. For each there is an event of creation, by some external force majeure, and then a gradual reversion to the status quo. Moreover, these histories are all unsymmetrical in the same direction of time, from which our idea of the 'arrow of time' pointing from past to future derives.

The external force always intervenes on the 'big bang' side of the sequence of events and the relapse always runs on towards the expanded universe side.

Smoothing down is only one of the ways in which chance makes itself felt in nature. Sometimes it is quite opposite and a single chance event changes the entire course of history. It is chance in this pioneering role that shakes the living world out of its grooves, through the mutation of the genetic molecule. Accidental strikes of radiation or contacts with chemicals at chance places along nucleic acid molecules have, over thousands of millions of years, thrown up all kinds of new candidates to compete in the great tournaments of natural selection; and year by year the standard of performance has gone up, all the way to today's sophisticated life. Because the mutations occur by blind chance, which upsets the otherwise routine flow of exact replication, the appearance of new strains is true creation, something completely 'out of the blue'. There *is* continuous creation in the world, if not of matter itself, certainly of the *organisation* of matter.

There is no general direction to natural selection other than that of unfailing adaptation to the environment. Features that were a disadvantage in wet seasons become an advantage during drought, and vice versa. But classical biological evolution, a blind progression based on different abilities of organisms to produce survivable offspring, has now evolved its successor. For, with the mind of man has come conscious *purpose* which can shape future events to chosen goals. At its simplest and most direct, this appears in our replacement of natural selection by wilful plant and animal breeding. But this is trifling compared with the power of the general change. The development of advanced mental capabilities gave their possessors such enormous advantages that the evolution from hominid to modern man has been phenomenally fast. Furthermore, as the advantages of his innate mental powers were intensified through the sharing of ideas, experiences, knowledge and beliefs by means of intricate languages and children's education, evolution veered into a different direction altogether, that of *cultural* and *social* advance, unrelated to genetic change. Darwinian natural selection plays little part in the progress of mankind now, for this is dominated by our conscious striving towards personal satisfaction and social change. There is purpose in the world today, human purpose, and we have to find for ourselves the ability to handle our powers wisely. This message surely remains the same even for those who believe that our mental and spiritual attributes are divinely given – a belief that cannot be objectively refuted, so long as the understanding of the mind transcends the capabilities of the brain – for why should these attributes have been given to us, if not to be used self-reliantly?

The Subjective Outlook

However exactly and dispassionately we examine nature, with thermometers for finger tips, spectroscopes for eyes, what we see always depends on our point of view. Everything we know of nature comes in the end from our personal experiences or by hearsay from those of others. The position and influence of the observer can never be altogether ignored, so that there is always a subjective aspect to all we know. This is obvious in the psychological sciences but true also in the physical ones.

Copernicus exposed the egocentric parochialism that distorts our naive impressions of what we see, but it was Einstein who hammered home the modern relativistic outlook by demonstrating forcibly that one man's simultaneity may be another's lapse of time; one man's gravitation another's acceleration. Of course, even here we can still pretend that we are remote spectators who merely passively observe the world – admittedly from various points of view – without being engaged in its actions. But this last refuge of objectivity crumbles when we recall that we learn of nature through the signals it sends us and that a signal is a material thing, never smaller than one quantum of action. When we observe nature we are part of its processes. Of course in nature's big pageants such as a sunrise, lightning flash, or apple's fall, so much action goes on, compared with that needed to carry the news, that the appearance of objectivity is saved and we can reasonably regard ourselves as wholly outside the spectacle.

But we cannot help thinking subjectively even about nature in the large. Consider for example the 'irreversible' running-down processes associated with the second law of thermodynamics. Their basis is the restlessness of nature, the perpetual dance of atoms, molecules and quanta that carries all matter through a vast repertoire of different configurations. Any given arrangement of its particles exists for a fleeting moment and is then gone beyond recall, as the particles move on ceaselessly into the myriads of alternatives. In these individual fine-scale structures the system is never the same twice. This is the basic feature of irreversibility. However, to our blunt senses, enormous numbers of these fine structures look the same and, because their individuality escapes our notice, so also does their individual irreversibility. Still undisturbed air in a room seems to stay in the same state of uniformity and immobility, even though its molecules are continually exploring an enormous number of different fine structures. But if we start off with a system in a state of visibly unusual structures – for example by gathering all the air temporarily into one corner of the room – we would then notice the irreversibility since we would perceive the air's dispersal from its uneven distribution to a uniform one. For us, then, irreversibility is in the eye of the beholder, a subjective effect of the fact that some classes of fine-scale structures are unusual enough to impress themselves on our senses. Although subjective, it has real practical consequences since, where we can *see* that a system is in an unusual state, we can if we wish put paddles or pistons round it to make it do work for us as it reverts to ordinariness.

Atoms and molecules are of course often prevented, by the forces between them, from exploring all geometrically possible structures and so, particularly at low temperatures, crystals and other ordered states of systems are stable. The order in biological molecules is of a much more complex kind, the outcome of long evolution and dependent for its maintenance on a continual input of ordered energy from the world outside. The chance of a number of atoms accidentally coming together to make a man is of course completely negligible, but evolution has gone in steps, each small and not wildly improbable; and the long stretches of geological time have provided the opportunities for life to consolidate itself at every stage by mass-producing each successful new step throughout entire populations.

Biological evolution, through its use of creative opportunities opened up by chance, provides one of the most interesting and subtle examples of the arrow of time in the expanding universe. Of all physical aspects of the universe, time is perhaps that which we view most subjectively. We have an overwhelming personal sense of time flowing relentlessly forward, sweeping us all along together, and with only one small part of it, the 'present' or 'now', really accessible to us, for we can remember the past but not the future and can influence the future but not the past.

Some of this of course fits in with an objective picture of time. If our memory is a network of material links in the brain then it is in principle the same as the footprints in the sand, an enduring physical record of events which, for reasons we have already seen, can only be in the past, not the future. Furthermore, we ourselves have some ordered energy at our disposal which, like the kinetic energy of the meteorite approaching the moon, can be used to make a future mark on the world. But the ideas of the 'flow of time' and of 'now' seem altogether more subjective. At what rate does time flow? One second per second? What meaning can be attached to that? In nature all we find is merely a *sequence* of events and time is no more than the relation between them. Without events there is no time. The simultaneity of events is an objective feature of nature, which refers to events at the same place occurring at the same time. But nothing of 'now' appears in this until one of these simultaneous events is an event in our brain which rouses our conscious interest in time, for 'now' is the name we give fleetingly to that moment at which an event is occurring, in our minds, that is making us aware of time itself. And this name is transferred to a succeeding moment of time as soon as we realise that we are into another mental event. Because our mental events are linked by brain, senses and limbs to events in the world outside, and so to other people's mental events, which may all occur together, our 'now' may seem to be something objective because it gets mistakenly dressed in clothes belonging to 'simultaneity'.

Pictures in the Mind

There is an even deeper reason why the portrait of nature is so much a reflection of its painter. It reveals not only what we know, or think we know, but also what we understand. This understanding is our own creation, an imaginative interpretation of the knowledge in which we try to blend all the separate scraps of fact together into a single unified picture.

This is not something peculiarly scientific, but traditional. We all simply cannot help making pictures in our minds. Forming general ideas about the things round us is one of the activities which makes us what we are. A skewed pattern of light and colour comes into our eyes and we 'read' it to mean that, say, a table or chair is set before us at a certain angle. If this seems too trivial an example, we should remember that philosophy has been hard put to analyse it precisely, and also that it is very difficult to teach computers to read irregular patterns such as handwriting.

The understanding of the common experiences of our daily lives is done for us by our subconscious faculties, so effectively and with such little fuss, that we are usually unaware of it and think nothing of it. Indeed, we manage a lot of day-to-day business without the overt help of a general picture. Much ordinary activity can be run on a 'black box' basis; a catalogue, in the memory, of all the examples of 'when I do *this*, then *that* happens'. You do not need to know how a car works to be able to drive it, only that pulling particular knobs and levers does various known things to its performance. Again, you do not have to be a biologist to be a gardener; an empirical set of rules-of-thumb will get you a long way.

It has thus not been for the *applications* of knowledge that understanding has been needed – although it often helps, of course – but to satisfy man's deep longing to comprehend the world in which he finds himself. From their earliest days and however ill-prepared they were for the task, our ancestors must have formed some general pictures in their minds about the world, because once they could think consciously and coherently they could not leave it a total blank. Man's early images were of a world he feared, of malevolent spirits and angry gods which he tried to placate with sacrifices, but these visions slowly evolved and refined into the sublime concepts of the great religions, of a world of hope and faith and love, although some fears still remained, as Dante portrayed in his *Inferno*.

But then came the discovery, perhaps the greatest single thing we have learnt about nature, that questions we put to nature are *answered*, provided they are of the right kind – questions of *fact* – and are clearly expressed and expertly presented (all of which requires great skill, sometimes genius, and much patience and effort). As a result our picture today is enormously expanded, far beyond the facts of everyday experience, by all the knowledge gathered from scientific observation and experiment: the spectra of the stars, masses of elementary particles, energies of atoms, structures of molecules and crystals, shifting of continents, circulation of the blood, splitting of chromosomes, ages of fossils, to name but a few.

This influx of hard knowledge has been matched by a corresponding advance in our level of understanding, going forward from the direct realisations of everyday life and the beliefs of dogmatic religion to the disciplined, modest but clear understanding of theoretical science; the understanding for example of the fall of apples, motions of the moon and planets, rotations of double stars, and aspects of the structures of galaxies, all as examples of the general working of the inverse-square law of gravitation. Laws such as this win their spurs by rigorous testing and sceptical analysis, but they never entirely lose their tentative character, for they are man-made constructs, our own interpretations of nature, and even the best of them eventually fail when tested against all the new and ever more refined knowledge that continues to flow in from scientific enquiry, although even in failure they remain generally useful.

The scientific picture of nature in fact constantly changes as new knowledge is gained and new understanding grasped. We are continually getting new facts, such as the recent discoveries of universal microwave radiation, the drift of continents, and the structures of biological molecules; and improving our understanding of nature, as with the recent ideas about the cosmic direction of time, the material nature of information, and the molecular basis of genetics. Some things we know but do not yet fully, or in some cases even partly, understand: for example, the basis of the earth's magnetism, ball lightning, the masses of elementary particles, quasars, the differentiation of multiplying egg cells into bodily organs, the mechanisms of taste and smell, and many psychological happenings such as dreams and hypnotism. In other cases, for example black holes, quarks, memory molecules, even the facts are still in doubt, although these speculative objects stand at a far higher level of scientific credibility than, for example, flying saucers or occult phenomena.

Broadly, there are three things portrayed in the picture: the world of the very *large*, the cosmos; that of the very *small*, the elementary particles; and that of the very *complex*, all the middle-sized things from the sun and earth down to atoms and molecules, including man himself. If we probe deeply enough into each of these we find in the end that nature becomes so strange as to be almost incomprehensible. We meet the curvature of space and time, and the curious circularity of matter making the geometry and geometry making matter. We meet the mirage-like nature of elementary particles, some of which seem as incorporeal as the disembodied grin of the Cheshire Cat. And in the middle-sized world the strangest are the most intimate things of all, the self-awareness that each of us has, and the mysterious frontier along which the mental and physical worlds meet.

At the world of the mind our scientific picture reaches its limits. Admittedly, something can be said by psychology, linguistics and logic. But for further understanding here we have to turn to the arts and literature, to the great novelists with their insight into human nature, to Rembrandt and Michelangelo, and to the musicians who express human feelings directly. This kind of understanding, although not cast in scientific terms, at its best is intensely perceptive and exact, as we all know by direct personal experience of its effects. Perhaps it will be possible one day to paint the worlds of the arts and sciences all in the same picture, as foreseen by Ezra Pound in his words: 'the arts, literature, poesy, are a science just as chemistry is a science. Their subject is man, mankind and the individual'.

At this point of time, however, not even the physical picture is yet fully together. Many parts, such as atomic physics and chemistry, are of course now well joined; but, on the other hand, the quantum properties of matter seem quite disconnected from the gravitational properties. It is probable that a greater common understanding still remains to be found, one that will link up the size of the universe, the speed of light, and the masses and numbers of the elementary particles, in a single unified concept. Perhaps we shall also see a relationship between the four fundamental forces of nature, and understand why time is so curiously like space yet so different. But, however far such grand syntheses may go, they will always leave something unexplained, for it is in the very nature of scientific explanation itself to explain things only in terms of other primary things that themselves lie outside the explanation. Science could thus never give a *total* account of the world. It must always leave a 'first cause' unexplained and so can never exclude the possibility of divine cause. If we wish to believe that God created the world – set it going, to find its own way along some indeterminate but physically lawful course – there is nothing in science to contradict this, nor can there be.

Between this last question and our present position the gap is indeed wide. But there is every likelihood that it will continue to close, for there seems no limit to nature's responsiveness to good and well presented questions. And it is deep in our own natures to seek enlightenment about the world and our place in it, and to be exhilarated by its magnificent and challenging answers.

INDEX